PRAISE FOR *THE SAFE LIBRARY*

"I have used Dr. Albrecht on numerous occasions for special training programs and found his workshops and books to be invaluable tools for libraries. *The Safe Library* can help you thoroughly examine how your library can address many of the old and new safety and security issues amplified by the pandemic, and the divisive behaviors that library boards, administration, and employees are sometimes dealing with on a daily basis from their users. Every library should invest in a copy of this book for their internal professional collection for their organization."

—**Andrew Sanderbeck**, trainer and consultant for libraries, founder, PCI Webinars, Largo, Florida

"Steve is a library security professional and a skilled collaborator. He presents thought-provoking ideas on making libraries safe, and his book is a practical tool for all library staff. Steve does not reinvent the wheel; he looks at all the wheels and brings those ideas together for the benefit of everyone. If you are working on safety and security in any library, public, private, law, or academic, you need this book, not on the shelf, but on your desk as a reference. It's worth the time to read it, and the ideas inside just may save a life."

—**Chester Price**, safety and security manager, emergency coordinating officer, Jacksonville Public Library, Jacksonville, Florida

"As the world has been thrown into turmoil because of the pandemic, so have been libraries, librarians, and our patrons. Librarians have found themselves thrust into situations where while working in a state of crisis they are also desperately needed to provide for their patrons who are also in crisis. This has created environments of heightened stress and increases in the need for all library staff and stakeholders to do whatever possible to increase safety for all. Steve has become an expert in this area and addresses this with solid, practical descriptions and actionable advice for all libraries. This timely book is an essential read."

—**Cindy Grove**, director, Rockport Public Library, Rockport, Massachusetts

The Safe Library

The Safe Library
Keeping Users, Staff, and Collections Secure

Steve Albrecht

ROWMAN & LITTLEFIELD
Lanham • Boulder • New York • London

Published by Rowman & Littlefield
An imprint of The Rowman & Littlefield Publishing Group, Inc.
4501 Forbes Boulevard, Suite 200, Lanham, Maryland 20706
www.rowman.com

86–90 Paul Street, London EC2A 4NE

Copyright © 2023 by The Rowman & Littlefield Publishing Group, Inc.

Author's Note
None of what you read here should be perceived as legal, medical, or mental health advice. As always, when it comes to legal, medical, or mental health issues or questions, consult a licensed attorney, a licensed physician, and/or a licensed clinician.

All rights reserved. No part of this book may be reproduced in any form or by any electronic or mechanical means, including information storage and retrieval systems, without written permission from the publisher, except by a reviewer who may quote passages in a review.

British Library Cataloguing in Publication Information Available

Library of Congress Cataloging-in-Publication Data Available

ISBN 978-1-5381-6959-9 (cloth)
ISBN 978-1-5381-6960-5 (paper)
ISBN 978-1-5381-6961-2 (electronic)

To my parents, Eileen Hodes and Karl Albrecht, who took me to libraries on Saturdays, nurtured my lifelong love of books, and always encouraged me to think, read, and write.

My work in libraries is greatly enhanced by the support of librarians around the country who have shared their security concerns, educated me on the daily operations at their facilities, and allowed me to talk to their staffs in ways that helped us all. This was especially true during the significant challenges caused by the international COVID-19 crisis, from 2020 to 2022.

Thanks to all of the library directors who had the kindness and courage to allow me to get in front of their employees and say my words about service, safety, and security.

And to all those library staff members who sat patiently and participated in my programs, took what I said, applied it in their situations, and tried to prove me right with my tools, suggestions, and methods, I thank you.

Contents

Acknowledgments — xi
Introduction — xv

Chapter 1: What They Don't Teach You in Library School: Security Matters, Talking Helps — 1

Chapter 2: Training Library Staff in Service, Safety, and Security: Focus on the Need Premise — 15

Chapter 3: Preventing Harassment of Library Staff: Responding to Sexual or Racial Behaviors by Patrons — 29

Chapter 4: Better Responses for Patrons Dealing with Homelessness: An Empathy-Driven Understanding — 37

Chapter 5: Dealing with Patrons with Mental Health and Substance Use Disorders: Behavioral and Medical Events — 49

Chapter 6: The Top Ten Most Challenging Patrons — 65

Chapter 7: Working Safely in a Rural Location: The One-Employee or Micro-Staff Library — 85

Chapter 8: An Armed Attacker in the Library: Rare, Catastrophic, and Survivable — 99

Chapter 9: The Need for New Responses at Your Library: Police Officers and Security Guards — 109

Chapter 10: A Plan for Library Emergencies:
Medical Events, Fires, and Beyond   121

Appendixes: Additional Security Tools   135
Appendix A: Sample Security Incident Report Format   137
Appendix B: Inspection Days   139
Appendix C: The Need for a Visitor/Vendor Access Policy   143
Appendix D: The Perils of the Parking Lot   147
Appendix E: Safe Library Events   153
Index   161
About the Author   171

Acknowledgments

People mostly read this part of a book to see if their name is included, not because it matters much to them otherwise. I was told once by a famous author always to put as many people as you know into this section so that they will feel compelled, stimulated, or guilted into buying a copy of the book. I am not that manipulative. I do hope the people that I have recognized in my list of colleagues and clients here will know the value they have brought to my professional life as a library security consultant. (And if their friends, colleagues, or children buy the book for them as a holiday or birthday present, that's okay too.)

Many of my webinar hosts have been helpful to me, but none more than my training partner and marketing genius, Steve Hargadon, founder of Library 2.0 (www.Library20.com). He has managed the platforms for my webinars, articles, and podcasts for many good and productive years. His wisdom and support as a sounding board for our various projects together are second only to the two facts that he is both a good man and a trusted friend.

Nick Hedrick, formerly the training specialist for the San José Public Library, in San José, California, has championed my work for his city well above any necessity on his part. I value his friendship and his concern for the employees in his city.

Andrew Sanderbeck, founder of PCI Webinars (People Connect Institute) and his staff, including Anne and Brian, have always championed my ideas in their online programs.

Vikki McLean, from the Tampa Bay Library Consortium, is a source of support and is always of good cheer.

Cindy S. Church, continuing education consultant for the State of Virginia, shepherded several library training programs for me around her state. I have promised her never to act like another author she worked with, who earned the reputation of being diva-esque and difficult.

Thanks and a hearty "Go Orioles!" to my Maryland colleague, Dr. Jennifer Hopwood, training and development specialist from the Southern Maryland Regional Library Association. She has been an invaluable resource for Steve Hargadon and me. Maryland, of course, is the state with the best crab cakes.

My thanks to Marylanders Jenny Newman, executive director of LibraryWorks, and Mary Herdoiza, program manager at LibraryWorks. Both ladies always got me to the right place and time for our webinars.

Joseph Filapek, director of consulting and continuing education, and Mary Louise Svehla, consulting and continuing education specialist, both from Reaching Across Illinois Library System (RAILS), have always been good shepherds of my webinars for them.

Thanks to Dan Freeman, director of ALA (American Library Association) Publishing's eLearning Solutions, for his support of my webinar programs for more than a decade. Kudos to Dan's assistant, master organizer, and technical wizard at the ALA, Colton Ursiny. He always manages to make my webinars look and sound professional.

Thanks to Chester Price, manager for safety and security at the Jacksonville, Florida, Public Library System, for his contribution to this book via the "Event Emergency Plan" template. His comprehensive planning document filled a gap in my knowledge that existed for too many years and yet is so simple and necessary. If you plan to have an event at your library that involves more than your usual number of kids or adults, you have to create a safety and security plan to cover the possible issues you may face pertaining to emergency evacuations, group safety, and the like. Use Chet's design for your events.

Thanks to fellow ALA author Ryan Dowd for his friendship and advice about a tough subject, where he is the better expert than I. His 2018 ALA book, *The Librarian's Guide to Homelessness*, should be required reading for every library employee who deals with this challenging and changing population.

Thanks to good friend Maurice Coleman (www.ColemanAssociates.net), a longtime Maryland library professional (and long-suffering New York Giants fan), for his support and contribution to my knowledge of diversity, equity, and inclusion in the library world, both for patrons and staff.

And thanks to the many library directors, program managers, training managers, library consultants, and staffs of state, public, special, and law libraries around the United States where I brought either my one- to four-hour webinars or my half-day training program into their facilities (listed below). I have always appreciated your kind words, feedback, questions, and good library jokes. For example, "How many librarians does it take to change a light bulb? Wait here while we look that up for you."

Ann Marie Creegan, Arizona State Library Archives and Public Records; Phoenix, Arizona
Beatriz Sarmiento, Library Director, City of Commerce Public Library; Commerce, California
Misty Jones, Library Director, City of San Diego Library; San Diego, California
Special Libraries Association
Colorado State Library Association
Massachusetts State Library Association
Watertown Library; Watertown, Wisconsin

Bridges Library System; Waukesha, Wisconsin
Alameda County Public Library; Alameda, California
Montgomery County (Maryland) Library
Cumberland County (Pennsylvania) Library
Downer's Grove Library; Downer's Grove, Illinois
Scituate Library; Scituate, Massachusetts
Georgia Public Library Service; Atlanta, Georgia
Texas State Library and Archives Commission; Austin, Texas
Bay County Library System; Bay City, Michigan
Southeast Florida Library Information Network; Boca Raton, Florida
City of Burlingame Public Library; Burlingame, California
City of Carson City Public Library; Carson City, Nevada
Southern Maryland Regional Library Association; Charlotte Hall, Maryland
American Association of Law Libraries; Chicago, Illinois
Indianhead Federated Library System; Eau Claire, Wisconsin
Otsego County Public Library; Gaylord, Michigan
Crandall Public Library; Glens Falls, New York
Nicolet Federated Library System; Green Bay, Wisconsin
Central Kansas Library System; Great Bend, Kansas
Western Maryland Regional Libraries; Hagerstown, Maryland
Hudson Library and Historical Society; Hudson, Ohio
Midwest Collaborative for Library Services; Lansing, Michigan
Thomas Branigan Memorial Library; Las Cruces, New Mexico
Long Beach Public Library; Long Beach, California
Massachusetts Library Association; Malden, Massachusetts
Murietta Public Library; Murietta, California
North Kansas City Public Library; North Kansas City, Missouri
Enlow Public Library; Oakland, Maryland
Oceanside Public Library; Oceanside, California
Southern Tier Library System; Painted Post, New York
Panhandle Library Access Network; Panama City Beach, Florida
Poughkeepsie Public Library District; Poughkeepsie, New York
North Carolina Department of Natural and Cultural Resources; Raleigh, North Carolina
Rancho Cucamonga Library; Rancho Cucamonga, California
Sacramento County Law Library; Sacramento, California
San Leandro Public Library; San Leandro, California
Infopeople / Califa Group; San Mateo, California
Santa Cruz Public Library; Santa Cruz, California
Live Oak Public Library; Savannah, Georgia
Northland Pioneer College Library; Show Low, Arizona
South Pasadena Public Library; South Pasadena, California
Inland Northwest Council of Libraries; Spokane, Washington

Tacoma Public Library; Tacoma, Washington
Leroy Collins Branch, Leon County Public Library; Tallahassee, Florida
Tampa Bay Library Consortium; Tampa, Florida
North Central Library District; Williamsport, Pennsylvania
North Star Borough Library, Fairbanks, Arkansas
Troy Library; Troy, Michigan
Royal Oak Library; Royal Oak, Michigan
Baton Rouge Library; Baton Rouge, Louisiana
Springfield-Greene County Library District; Springfield, Missouri
City and County of San Luis Obispo (California) Libraries
Princeton Library; Princeton, New Jersey
Athens Library; Athens, Georgia
Topeka Library; Topeka, Kansas
Sacramento Library; Sacramento, California
Little Rock Library; Little Rock, Arkansas
County of Erie (Pennsylvania) Library
County of Placer (California) Library
Independent Cities Risk Management Association; Irvine, California
SEFLIN (Southeast Florida Library Information Network)
NEFLIN (Northeast Florida Library Information Network)
State of Maryland Library
State of Kansas Library
State of Washington Library
State of Ohio Library
State of Louisiana Library
State of Idaho Library
State of New Jersey Library
State of Utah Library

Introduction

What a difference two years makes, eh? As I write this in the late summer of 2022, we have just come out of a global pandemic that started in March 2020 and was not previously experienced in the United States since 1918. Suffice to say we have all seen, heard, done, and had quite enough of COVID-19, aka the Coronavirus.

During that time, we also saw some of the most serious protests about race and police misconduct in our country, not witnessed since 1968 (during the Martin Luther King and Robert F. Kennedy murders) and 1992 (the Rodney King riots in Los Angeles). Both of these events have affected the words you see here. We need to be different in how we think about how we serve all of our patrons. We need to think differently about how we protect our facilities from threats that could come from people, viruses, and even from the cyber world. We need to have better relationships and good boundaries when it comes to the police response to our libraries. We will always need the police, but we won't always need the police in our libraries, if that makes sense. There is a time when their response is vital and life saving, and there are times library leaders and staffers can handle things themselves. I'll talk more about working effectively with law enforcement (and maybe some things you don't know about the police culture, which might help you understand their methods), using more positive liaison opportunities, and how to rebuild community and library employee trust with them.

I wrote this book to help library leaders and frontline library employees create a safer, more secure workspace by providing realistic, viable, and field-tested tools for dealing with challenging or problematic patrons. I know this to be true because in my role as one of the leading national experts on library safety and security issues, I have learned quite a lot from the thousands of library professionals who have attended my training workshops. This book is the result of my work teaching in-person programs and conducting webinars for libraries around the United States since 2000. I have learned a lot in twenty-two years. And as a guy who is not a library professional, I still feel qualified to speak on protecting libraries, employees, and patrons because of my exposure to so many outstanding employees working in facilities both large and small (rural, suburban, and urban; city and county public, law, and special libraries) and my observations of so many of their interactions with all types of patrons (both the positive ones and the ones that didn't go so well).

Many people who started working at libraries probably first thought it was about being around great books and periodicals. They quickly discovered that library work is really about people and, in many cases, interesting, pleasant, thankful, eccentric, rude, entitled, fascinating, obnoxious, demanding, or needy people.

The position of the library as a focal point for public use has evolved in many communities. Back "In The Good Old Days at the Library," as I often say when I recall the past, the main educational programs at most libraries had to do with formalized, structured adult literacy training meetings and children's programs, designed to expose them to the magic of books and the other treasures in the library. I know this because I was a Library Kid and I convinced my daughter to become a Library Kid at a tender age as well.

Today, the public library features the same adult literacy and children's programs, but with so much more. This includes providing access to volunteer lawyers who can give legal aid services to citizens who need it; access to meeting rooms, training rooms, and auditoriums for community, civic, and special-interest groups who rent them for their groups (I've seen Alcoholics Anonymous meetings held in library meeting rooms); LGBTQ meetings and support programs; "banned book and protected content" discussions; speeches made at libraries by local and national politicians; local and national authors on book tours; gardening clubs; space for quilters to unroll their work; tour stops in the library for historical artifacts, dinosaur bones, and famous artworks; and so many other programs, displays, meetings, and educational opportunities that bring people to libraries. Perhaps with all this, we continue our usual mission of convincing the library skeptics (who may vote no on future library funding, since they have no real idea what goes on in one) to stop saying, "What do we need a local library for, since everybody already has access to Google?"

People entering our public spaces—city halls, county administration buildings, courthouses, libraries—bring the possibility of conflict between them and the employees. If you've ever thought, "Why can't we pick our customers? Why can't we choose which patrons we let through the door for the day?" then you've probably had a long day on your feet, serving people who didn't always thank you for your efforts. As the Shepherds of the Public Library (more on this concept later), we get who we get. It's our job to create a safe, pleasant, service-oriented workspace for all who enter—and to maintain it every day we're open. This is easy to say and hard to do, sometimes.

Library staff continue to have to deal with patrons whose behavior can challenge even the most patient employee. This includes the entitled patron, who feels the Code of Conduct or policies don't apply to him or her; the chronically homeless patrons, who use the library as an all-day landing spot and often have substance abuse and mental illness issues; hostile teenagers; confused elderly or disabled patrons; thieves; vandals; gang members; and patrons who dominate or misuse the internet. And while certainly not all patrons are dangerous, some can use threatening words and behaviors to frighten staff and other visitors. Since libraries are not always high on the response priority for law enforcement, it's often up to the staff (first), their supervisors (second), and the library director (third) to create and maintain a safe library in the face of these patron challenges.

My approach to this book is twofold. I wrote it to appeal to library directors, managers, and supervisors, so they may follow the guidelines for physical security improvements, policy changes, and improvements to the Code of Conduct, and to help them help their people enforce their rules by seeing the book as a training guide for their staffs. I also wrote it to be readable, immediately useful, and valuable to frontline library employees, who can feel safer at work, more empowered with their own sense of security, and more comfortable dealing with challenging patrons during less-than-stellar behavioral situations. If you have worked at only one library or many, if you have worked at a library for two weeks or twenty years, if you are a full-time employee, part-timer, intern, volunteer, or student librarian, this book is for you. I hope your bosses will take what they need to keep you safe and you will apply the tools as you see fit.

In the seven years since I wrote my book *Library Security: Better Communication, Safer Facilities* (2015) for the American Library Association (ALA), I have learned many more things about libraries, their patrons, and the employees and leaders who operate libraries in our communities. In short, the library world has become more complex, tense, and in some cities even dangerous. Assaults and attacks on library staffs were rare when I began my training and security consulting work for libraries in 2000. Now library facilities and their staffs are dealing with some serious issues related to crime, violence, and safety. A few horrible examples include these:

A patron lit himself on fire and died in the downtown Des Moines, Iowa, library. A patron was kicked out of the Tallahassee, Florida, library and left the building and set a woman on fire at a Taco Bell across the street. (I know about the last incident because I was teaching my class there at the time.)

An active-shooter event left two female library employees dead in Clovis, New Mexico. A female library security officer was stabbed to death in Spring Valley, New York. A male library director was stabbed to death as he opened the building for a Saturday book fair in Fort Myers Beach, Florida. A female library manager was shot to death by a patron in the parking lot of a Sacramento, California, library. (This same person had been banned previously from several libraries in St. Louis, Missouri.)

Crime from the streets (theft, vandalism, assaults, violence) has entered some library branches in ways I did not fully anticipate seven years ago. Even intentional arson fires have found their way to the library space. In 2020, two thirteen-year-olds in Porterville, California, set an intentional fire on the second floor of the children's section of the library and burned the building to the ground, killing two local firefighters in the process.

During my conversations with library leaders and employees who attend my programs, I hear about shadow security problems like unreported sexual harassment of female staffers by male patrons and racial harassment of other patrons or staff members by racist patrons. Both issues make me furious, and I have devoted a chapter here to our necessary responses.

According to demographic hiring data from the ALA, the ratio of female library employees to male library employees is nearly 70 percent to 30 percent.[1] These numbers might be higher or lower where you work, but either way, they suggest that, like other professions dominated by women (real estate, human resources, teaching, psychotherapy), libraries employ women who get harassed. You have the right to work in a harassment-free environment, and our library leaders must make certain that's in place.

For your part, if you aren't in charge, you have to tell your director or supervisors (or HR, or your agency's attorney, using what we call "multiple channels of reporting") when you're being harassed or made to feel unsafe while doing your work. The simple reason for that is that we (the collective leadership "we," and I'm including myself here) can't fix what we don't know about. It takes Courage, with an intentional uppercase C, to report people or situations that are bothering you. You can't expect your library leaders to be everywhere and see everything; you have to be part of the solution, too, by notifying them so they support you by creating workable and consistent solutions.

Library employees, who have wearily identified themselves as "untrained social workers," must deal with some patrons who have a significant trauma history. Their background of abuse or exposure to violence as children can affect their in-public behavior as adults. Those patrons who have had several life problems that make them feel helpless and hopeless turn to the library for answers, social connection, and support.

We'll discuss the frustration that library professionals at all levels feel about the ever increasing homeless population on our streets (150,000 just in my former home state of California alone), some of whom enter our libraries with serious mental health issues and substance use disorder problems. With no promises for perfect solutions, I've devoted a chapter to these two health, safety, and security issues.

Just like there are no fast or easy answers to homelessness, there are no simple or inexpensive solutions to two of its related companions: mental health problems and substance abuse disorders. These three issues affect some of your patrons to the degree that their behavior problems become our behavioral problems. Certainly not all mentally ill people are dangerous, and not all dangerous people are mentally ill. All patrons have the right to be treated with dignity, respect, and fairness. But by law in all fifty states, when they become a danger to themselves (suicidal), a danger to others (violent or homicidal), or what clinicians call "gravely disabled," meaning the person's mental illness is severe enough to cause himself or herself physical harm, the police usually need to come to the library to take them for a mental health evaluation. Certain libraries may see this type of patron daily; others rarely.

A library director in the upper Midwest told me his facility collects and disposes of forty heroin needles per month. (It's hard to imagine anywhere else but a medical clinic having a similar issue.) What was not a problem before the national opiate epidemic—opiate addicts and fentanyl users overdosing in libraries or leaving their drug paraphernalia behind—is now a common event in some urban libraries. Supervisors and staff need to know more about how to safely deal with opiate users who are either under the influence of heroin or pain pills, or worse, in withdrawal from those drugs. Libraries need to make some careful ethical, legal, medical, and security decisions about whether to keep the life-saving drug Narcan on site, and what responsibilities the staff members who volunteer to use Narcan on an overdosing patron need to consider. With drugs come safety hazards, including fentanyl exposures, needle sticks, and blood-borne pathogens. Alcoholics and stimulant drug (most typically meth) users bring their own erratic and cyclical behavior issues to the library. They need to be managed in different ways than opiate users.

We'll look at my list of "Top Ten Most Challenging Patrons," and how I (and you helped me) came up with these goes back about 126 years to an Italian gardener who happened to be an economist.

In 1896, the Italian economist Vilfredo Pareto discovered that 80 percent of his peas came from 20 percent of his pea pods. He used this gardening ratio to suggest that 20 percent of effort in most things brings 80 percent of the results. This gets proven over and over again with human behavior: 80 percent of the patron problems in the library tend to be caused by only 20 percent of the patrons. For some situations (and perhaps in your library location), 95 percent of the problems tend to be caused by 5 percent of the patrons. Either way, it may be a small but impactful group of "Challenging Patrons" who show up too often in our Security Incident Reports (SIRs), police responses, and both formal and informal staff discussions.

My list of the Top Ten Most Challenging Patrons may be similar to yours. Depending on where you work and what your job is in the library, you may come across these patrons daily, frequently, rarely, or never. I've included the following:

The Lonely, Needy Patron
The Technologically Confused Patron
The Staring Patron
The Triple-E Patron(s) (Entitled, Eccentric, Exasperating), Who Ignore Our Rules
The Patron Who Purposely Displays Pornography
The Tweenaged / Problem Student / Young Bully Patron
The Angry Parent Patron

The Elderly, Disabled, Dependent Adult, or Developmentally Disabled Patron; or an Abuser of Those Patrons
The Patron Who Hogs the Internet
The Patron Who Protests about Books or Other Content

And how about our colleagues out in the countryside, desert, mountains, or at the seaside, in small towns and rural cities, where the library is a focal point housed in a tiny building? It's become clear to me that library employees who work in rural and small library locations feel especially vulnerable to security incidents because they work in one- or two-person facilities where the local law enforcement response may be up to two hours away. I'll provide a lot of ideas for self-sufficiency and self-protection, which come from my security workshops specifically designed for rural librarians. (These hardworking staffers often feel like they are the only "Shepherds of Their Building" and won't leave their facility in a dangerous situation, even when you and I would.) They tell me their directors don't always pay attention to their safety and security needs until after a frightening incident. In other words, as is all too common in our world, they make security changes and improvements to policies and equipment only after a serious event.

The list of possible safety and security problems that come with operating a publicly accessed building that's open upward of eighty hours per week means a lot of things can happen. Some library emergencies are rare and manageable; others are rare and catastrophic. Library directors, managers, supervisors, and staff must know their roles in dealing with building fires, active shooters, weather events, plumbing problems, power blackouts, other utility emergencies, pests, robberies, burglaries, IT attacks, bomb threats, needle sticks, first aid events, car accidents in the parking lot, slips and falls, protest and civil unrest outside, and media management concerns.

As you well know from your library work experience, no matter how brief or how long (and thanks for your dedication), this job is more about just books, periodicals, research, and providing information; it's all about the people, on both sides of the Reference or Information desks. Successful patron behavior management means we may have to spend a lot of time doing the best we can to "coach up" those patrons who will listen to us about complying with our Code of Conduct and the basic rules of civility in a public environment.

The best and most common compliments I get from library participants in my training programs are these: "You talk about stuff they didn't teach us in Library School" and "You give us tools that are practical, memorable, and easy to use."

A WORD ABOUT MY EDITORIAL CHOICES

Since this is not a textbook, but more of an action manual, I've chosen to write it in the first person, as if I'm talking to you, because I am and I want you to know that I am with you when it comes to feeling and staying safe at work. Contrary to what some of my critics have said or written about me (most of whom have never seen my presentations), I am not blinded by my previous law enforcement career when it comes to knowing how to treat people with dignity and empathy in the library environment.

I'm not pro-police and anti-patron. I strongly disagree that—as one group oddly portrayed me—"this particular author frequently gives workshops to public library staff and writes books on the topic of library security, perpetuating this carceral mentality." (I had to look that last part up, being a Bear of Very Small Brain. Is this group suggesting I want to put all problematic library patrons in jail? Of course not.) I want the same thing for you in your library—be it large or small; urban, suburban, or rural; brand new building or decades-old historical facility—a peaceful workday. It is peace that I seek for all of us, not "justice."

I'm both a believer in diversity, equity, and inclusion (DEI) programs and a trainer who uses them for my clients. And my skilled DEI training colleagues, who are people of color (POCs), continue to educate me on these important issues when we team-teach for libraries. This is not a book that touches on DEI as its central concept, except to say that I believe that I'm into fairness in these pages, and we have the duty as employees and as humans to treat every person—patrons and colleagues alike—with dignity, empathy, and patience. I have been accused of knowing nothing about diversity because I am an older male, and not a POC. I can only say that as a husband, father, and employer who enjoys a wide variety of personal and professional relationships with a huge range of people of every stripe, I'm not trying to speak for anyone other than myself. And as one of my DEI trainer friends puts it, "You don't have to have cancer to be a cancer doctor. You don't have to be a depressed therapist to treat depression. We all come from our own way of seeing the world, and with time, and enlightenment, that view changes."

As consumers of words, providers of books and periodicals, and advocates for their fair and free access and use, some librarians—who have attended my training programs, read my articles or blogs, or listened to my library podcasts—have strong opinions about my use of "labels" to describe patrons. This includes my calling a patron who is experiencing homelessness a "homeless patron" or a "homeless person." Although they would prefer I call them "the unhoused" or "the unhomed," it's unwieldy for me as a writer to refer to them this way since these are phrases I have never heard until recently (and these are also phrases that people who are actually living on the streets don't use to refer to themselves).

I get that Language Matters. I'd prefer to follow the most common editorial practice of using "he or she" to describe people, instead of "they" (the preferred pronoun for some, based on the Twitter profiles I see). Please don't take offense; I'm trying to stay consistent.

Introduction

I understand that some library staff would prefer me to call patrons with mental illness issues as "having mental health challenges." Or they would rather I described patrons who use drugs and alcohol before or while at the library, and become difficult to deal with as their sobriety fades, as having "a substance use disorder" (SUD).

Please note that I am not now or ever value-judging these patrons (homeless, drug/alcohol addicted, mentally ill) for their life burdens. I'm not using labels; I'm most often trying to accurately describe their behaviors while in your presence. I will say it here and again over and over (and you can quote me on this): "I don't care what people look like; I only care what people do. And I only care about what they do if it impacts the business of your library in a negative way." In other words, don't confuse my other words if they are different than the ones you choose. Let's focus on creating a safe, secure, peaceful, and productive library everyone can enjoy.

You may see me use the phrase, "In my Perfect Library World (PLW) . . ." when I'm describing what I'd like to see for your library, if money and some hard-to-change policies were not restricting factors. These are what I hope/wish my libraries could aspire to, which may not ever be possible or not possible until sometime later. Don't be discouraged if my version of the Perfect Library World doesn't match yours quite yet. Do what you can do to get in the vicinity of it.

I wrote this book in the first person, so I can have a conversation with you about the incidents and events, patrons and problems, and libraries and librarians I have heard, seen, and met over the last twenty-plus years of my security consulting career. This book is not designed to be a dry textbook. I'd like to think I have a better-than-average sense of humor and I hope that comes out on these pages. We can talk about serious subjects in an empowering and even entertaining way. I'm with you, on these pages, and in spirit in your library.

YOUR TAKEAWAYS

For library leaders: This includes you if you're an executive director, library director, library board member, department head, manager, supervisor, PIC (person in charge), or lead employee. Take what you need to help you with coaching, training, new-employee orientation, and refreshers. Be ready to formulate new policies, train to them, model the ideas you like, and help staff put the tools to use. Maximize your leverage to help your employees and patrons stay safe.

For library employees: This includes you if you're a full-time employee, longtime employee, new employee, nearing-retirement employee, just-starting employee, a part-time employee, a volunteer, or an intern. Take what you need from me, my advice and examples (which you should share with colleagues and supervisors, if they meet your definition of "best practices"), and especially from the role-play scenarios found in several parts of this book. There is "no one perfect approach" to dealing with people in low- and high-stress service situations. Follow your intuition, know your policies, and get early help. Improvise! Adapt! Succeed!

NOTE

1. https://www.ala.org/pla/sites/ala.org.pla/files/content/data/PLA_Staff_Survey_Report_2022.pdf. Page 6.

1

What They Don't Teach You in Library School

SECURITY MATTERS, TALKING HELPS

On a break from teaching my half-day workshop, "Library Security: Dealing with Challenging Patrons," at one of the many libraries I have visited across the United States, a participant will come up to me and say, "The information you're giving us is stuff they sure didn't teach us in library school." Sometimes the staffers will say this to me with a gleam in their eyes, as if they are learning the secrets to success; other times it's a more rueful comment, as if they had missed out on some useful things prior to now.

I have heard variations of this same comment many times, and it goes back to a point I made in the 2015 ALA (American Library Association) edition of *Library Security*, which is this job is more than just books, periodicals, research, and providing information; it's all about people, on both sides of the desk.

ALA demographic data about library directors and gender suggests that about 65 percent are female and about 35 percent are male. These numbers are about the same for library employees, with some ratios in some systems or branches as high as 80 to 85 percent female and 15 to 20 percent male. It may be different where you are, but these numbers reflect the national average.[1]

It should come as no surprise that men and women see safety and danger differently. Ask the average guy when he felt afraid of being assaulted and he might say, "Back in high school, or at this bar, back in college, or there was this guy who came up to me at a gas station and got too close to me once." Ask the average woman the same question (and I include my adult daughter in this answer) and she will say, "Last night, as I was leaving the grocery store, I saw this guy start to follow me and I thought . . ."

Female staffers frequently tell me they are uncomfortable, anxious, afraid, and even threatened by the behaviors of certain male or female patrons that their male colleagues are not. This can lead to a disconnect in the response by male coworkers, supervisors, or managers, who don't see the urgency of the situation or think the patron's behavioral outburst was "no big deal." I tell all library employees, at every level, that it's okay to follow your intuition, to listen to the "little voice" in your head that is trying to tell you what to do to stay safe in all situations. I tell female employees not to rely exclusively on the judgment of their male coworkers and to make their own good decisions based on what works for them, first.

I define this personal responsibility as staying in Condition Yellow. This means when you are coming to and leaving work, or in any part of the library facility, you're paying attention to the patrons around you. Condition Yellow is the middle level of awareness. When you are moving across the library space, your eyes are up and moving, not looking at your phone or your papers. When you are working a desk, you look up from your screen regularly to see what is going on around you. Condition Yellow is your default posture, all your working day.

You move up to Condition Red when you need to flee a dangerous situation or protect yourself if that's not possible (flight or fight). You can move down a level, to Condition White, when it's safe to do so. This includes taking a bathroom or coffee break in the back office, eating your lunch with your colleagues in the employees-only break room, and arriving back home from work. When you are safely off the public floor, you can let your guard down in Condition White and recharge your batteries.

Condition Yellow is your preferred "public face" and the mode you need to stay in, where you have constant awareness about your personal space and professional boundaries.

DR. STEVE'S "ESSENTIAL EIGHT"

Let's consider my "Essential Eight." This list describes our need to treat all patrons the same way—with dignity, courtesy, and patience, even if we don't get that back from them. We don't care what they look like; we only care what they do and if what they do hurts our business or impacts the business of the library in a negative way, and we have to address it, alone or working with colleagues or bosses. Let's fully define each of my Essential Eight concepts, which can be abstract in principle but easy to operationalize and make more behaviorally concrete when we treat all patrons using this guide. Are we using these eight when it comes to patron treatment and interactions?

Firm—We apply our Code of Conduct and behavioral policies with an assertive posture.

Fair—We treat every patron fairly, without judging how they look, only how they act. If it doesn't hurt the business of the library, we move on with our other work activities. If a patron's behavior interferes with the safety and enjoyment of the library for others, we address it. Do we treat each person who is violating the policy the same, regardless of their age, race, gender, sexual orientation, disabilities, housing status, and so on?

Consistent—We apply our Code of Conduct and behavioral policies evenly, uniformly, and the same for every patron, every day. We shouldn't operate the library one way Monday, Tuesday, and Wednesday and differently Thursday, Friday, and Saturday. We don't enforce our Code of Conduct and behavioral policies for the first half of the week and not during the other half. Besides that it's not the way to run the library, when word gets out (and it always does, with disruptive teenagers, mentally ill homeless people, drug users, and troublemakers) that the library staff is vigilant only part of the week, then you will have behavioral problems for the entire week. We aren't running a prison camp, but we have a duty to care for every patron by providing a safe-use facility.

Legal—Are we up to date on any new legal issues about how patrons use our facilities? Service animals? Disability access? Internet access? Are our policies current? Have they been reviewed and vetted by our agency attorney? Are we providing fair, nondiscriminatory services to all patrons? Are we legally justified to ask patrons to leave for the day, give them a trespass warning, or ban them for a week, a year, or forever?

Assertive—Have we stepped up our conversational approach to be more assertive, especially with patrons who are entitled, demanding, impolite, rude, uncaring about the limits of the services we can provide, or dismissive of our rules of conduct? Assertive is not aggressive, and it's not passive either. It suggests you take control of the conversation and strive for outcomes you and the patron can agree upon.

Empathic—Empathy is different than sympathy. Being sympathetic to someone's plight or problems can cause you to become overly emotional and lose perspective. Empathy means you recognize the person is in pain or emotional discomfort and you can see clearly how it is impacting him or her. That approach makes it easier for you to help people who are struggling with various life issues without getting "caught up in their drama."

Patient—This is also tied to another crucial component—professional listening skills. The best customer service employees have it. They can hear the patron fully, without being distracted by phones, calls, paperwork, or other people. They listen fully and intently, and wait until the other person has finished before they respond (or they know how to interrupt a long-winded ramble with politeness and skill). They ask open-ended questions to get more information and closed-ended questions to get to the point and wrap it up. They take notes, as needed, to make certain they don't lose important details. They paraphrase back what they have heard, which demonstrates to the other person that they were actually listening. They seek solutions that work for the other person, and not just themselves.

Reasonable—The concept of reasonableness is a court-tested idea that appears many times in the law. Was this company reasonable in its hiring practices? Did this city or county do reasonable things when handling this taxpayer's complaint? In the library the question is similar: Are we being reasonable in how we enforce our Code of Conduct and behavioral policies?

DR. STEVE'S "CRITICAL CORE TEN"

What's the best thing to do when faced with a challenging patron? It depends. What's the best thing to do with a tough service situation? It depends. What's the best thing to do when faced with a potentially dangerous situation? It depends.

I'm not being a smarty pants; I'm being a consultant. ("It depends" is one of our favorite non-answer answers, especially when we don't know the actual answer.) Consider my Critical Core Ten as you assess your interactions with all patrons who draw your attention.

Like the Essential Eight, this list of ten is important for most patron interactions. It needs to be viewed as operational more than abstract. You don't need to put these on a laminated card and review them as you stand in front of a patron. (Hey! Maybe I'm onto something there.) As you get more experience thinking about them, you can run through these ten quickly and make skilled decisions. In any event involving patron behavior, ask yourself these ten questions:

1. What does my intuition tell me to do? (Listen to the Little Voice in your head.)
2. What does common sense suggest I do (or not do). (Not everything needs a response from you).
3. What is the impact on the business of our library? (No impact, low impact, or high impact?)
4. What does our Code of Conduct allow or prohibit? (You should know your Code backward and forward.)
5. What do our policies and training say I need to do? (What have I been instructed to do?)
6. What is our usual approach to this situation, based on the work culture we've created here? (Your rural library will have a different work culture than a downtown library. What you do in a big-city library may be the same or different than in a small-town library. Follow your work culture accordingly.)
7. Are we following the Essential Eight guidelines (mentioned earlier)?
8. Has there been a violation of local, city, county, state, or federal laws? (Penal Code, municipal code, health code [Hello Coronavirus!], or civil code? Read chapter 5 for my description of a Welfare and Institutions–type code commonly used to assess the mental health of a troubled or troubling person.)
9. Is it a medical issue? Mental health issue? Security guard issue? Police issue? Another agency issue? (Who else needs to respond, if any?)

10. Is there a creative, outside-the-box solution? (What can you or your colleagues and/or your boss come up with that solves everyone's issues in a calm, fair, and useful way?)

Are we seeing a pattern here? There are no perfect answers because we are dealing with imperfect people who may act in highly imperfect ways. Think on your feet, trust your intuition, and consider my Essential Eight and the Critical Core Ten as you decide what to do.

LET'S TALK ABOUT TALKING

I'm reminded of two useful books I like to recommend in my training programs, both related to having difficult or stressful conversations. The first is *Crucial Conversations* by Joseph Grenny, Kerry Patterson, Al Switzler, and Ron McMillan (2002).[2] All four authors are management consultants who set about studying why people have hard conversations, when they turn that way, and how to do them better.

The second book is *Verbal Judo* by the late Dr. George Thompson (1993; updated in 2013).[3] Thompson founded the Verbal Judo Institute (www.Verbal Judo.com), which is still training people today.

One of the things that we think about in dealing with angry people is how important it is to demonstrate empathy. In both books, the authors talk a lot about the critical value of empathy as one of the strongest tools we have to demonstrate not only the ability to listen to people who are upset but also to hear them where they are. Dr. George Thompson talks specifically about the opposite of empathy, which happens when we say, "Calm down!" to patrons who aren't in control. He says one of the reasons the phrase makes people so upset is that when we say "calm down," what it really means is, "I don't give you the right to be mad." It minimizes or subverts the person's ability to be mad, and he or she may have a legitimate reason to be angry.

If you've used the phrase before, I'll suggest boldly it has never worked for you. Saying "calm down" to somebody just pushes their hot buttons, and even people who are mild mannered and don't typically lose their temper will just go off when we say it to them. Thompson said instead of saying "calm down" to someone who is angry, try saying some variations of these empathy-building statements:

"I hear you."
"I hear what you're saying."
"I can see you're upset."
"It's going to be all right."
"I'm working on it."
"Let's figure out what to do."
"It's going to be okay."

"I've got some answers for you."

"You told me what I need to work on. You told me what I need to do. I'm going to do that on your behalf. I'm going to do that for you."

If you take nothing from this discussion about talking with patrons, please take "Calm down!" out of your communications toolbox forever.

Besides empathy as a big driver for our discussion here, another useful tool is patience. One of the reasons we're such poor listeners—and I put myself in that category from time to time as well—is that instead of hearing the other person, we're just waiting for them to stop talking so we can get our perspective across. If you've ever had a conversation with a friend, a colleague, or a loved one who doesn't let you finish and chops off the end of your words so they can get their words in, it's beyond frustrating.

Especially for people who are really upset, it serves you both better to let them finish, without interruption. Not only does waiting allow you to think of the things that you want to say, to come up with an answer, or devise a useful solution to what's concerning them, it's also respectful.

Right after his *Verbal Judo* book came out in 1993, I took one of Thompson's full-day courses in San Diego. I distinctly remember he said then that "difficult people are as eager to argue with you as nice people are to cooperate with you." That's a fairly provocative statement, right? I'll say it again: "Difficult people are as eager to argue with you as nice people are to cooperate with you." This reminds me of a concept therapists use to explain when their clients lash out at others, especially those trying to help them: "Hurt people hurt people."

When I first started dealing with angry and threatening people as part of my work in my career I figured out there were three types of folks in the world: "Yes" people, "Maybe" people, and "No" people. "Yes" people are cooperative. You could say, "May I ask you to wait over there for a moment while I research your information for you?" and they will do it. "Maybe" people say to themselves, "Maybe I will and maybe I won't. What's in it for me?" You can tell by their body language this is what they're thinking. So you say, "I need to step in the back for a moment. I need to go pull your information, and then I'll come back and take a quick look at the computer. It's going to take about five minutes. Could I ask you to wait over here?" After getting a fuller explanation, they'll probably cooperate.

The third person and the most difficult group of all is the "No" person. No matter what you tell them or how politely or fully you explain it, they're not going to do it; they're not going to cooperate. In public service work, you have to make a pretty quick assessment: are you dealing with a "Yes" person, a "Maybe" person, or a "No" person? It's difficult to deal with "No" people in general, but here's the problem: sometimes we turn "Yes" people and "Maybe" people into "No" people based on how we treat them and how we communicate with them. That's why we've been talking about these tools from both books. Do whatever you can to keep "Yes" people from becoming "No" people because you were not empathic or patient, and failed to adequately explain your actions to them.

The four consultants who wrote *Crucial Conversations* said that 90 percent of the time we have routine, casual, normal conversations with people at home and work and we do fine at them. But for about 10 percent of our conversations, we blow it. We get angry, we argue with people, we lose control, we have emotional issues, we get frustrated, we get anxious, we get fearful, and somehow the conversation does not go as well as those other 90 percent. The difference between the 90 percent talks and the 10 percent talks is three critical (or in their parlance, crucial) concepts that arise for one or both people: high stakes, strong emotions, and different opinions as to what to do. If you look at conversations with your kids, your spouse or partner, your parents, or your boss and those three elements apply, it can suddenly turn into a Crucial Conversation.

With this three-part definition in mind—high stakes, strong emotions, and different opinions as to what to do—look back on those conversations in the library where you were in conflict with a patron. Suffice to say that while that discussion/argument/shouting match might not have been that important to you, to the patron it was crucial. Let's combine all three in a scenario that's probably common in your library.

The patron needs to create a resume, which he has never done, to apply for a new job online, which he has also never done, using an e-mail address that he does not have. High stakes!

The patron is fearful, anxious, and irritated that you may not be able to do all this for him because you're busy with other patrons and he is facing a 4:30 p.m. deadline to submit these documents to the prospective employer, and oh, by the way, you get off work at 4:00 and it's 3:30. Strong emotions!

You tell the patron you can help him only so much before you have to leave for the day. Could he come in early tomorrow? No! Can you give him a cheat sheet or a template for resume creation? No! Can you ask him to wait until another coworker is free to help, probably about 4:30? No! Different opinions as to what to do!

What seems like Just Another Day at the Library for you is a Significant Day for the patron. There is a disconnect—not your fault, to be sure—about the importance of his tasks versus what you can help him with. We have all the ingredients for a Crucial Conversation, and that's when the talk can turn intense.

The authors make two points: recognizing when a conversation turns crucial is Job One for you; having the right tools to handle a crucial conversation when you discover it is Job Two. I highly recommend the book and the authors' accompanying YouTube videos about the crucial conversations concept.

NEUTRAL BODY LANGUAGE, SHAME, AND EMBARRASSMENT

When we examine the way human beings communicate, so much of it is nonverbal. There's some old statistic floating around that suggests about 60 percent of the way we communicate is nonverbal, 30 percent is verbal, and the other 10 percent is who knows what. Who knows if that's true but it sounds correct. So much of what we do involves our eyes and eyebrows, our face and mouth, and our hands and arms. Consider the extreme difference between standing in a neutral posture, with just your hands at your sides or hands by your waist in a relaxed position versus having both arms crossed, rolling your eyes, sighing, looking at your watch or your phone, and tightening your lips in that way that says to the other person, "I'm bored."

Know it or not and like it or not, many patrons in the library read you all the time. They're watching you before they come and talk to you to see if you look approachable. They gauge how you handle other people asking for help. They look to see how you handle certain patron behavioral situations. It's important that we don't come across as bored robots, that we display an open posture and open body language, and that we make polite eye contact with everyone in a respectful way.

It's really important to understand that certain patrons you talk to may be anxious, frustrated, angry, or even rageful about the situation they find themselves in. You need to be able to recognize those emotions when you see them, when they are overt for sure, but even more so when the person is trying to hide them. Some patrons show their emotions assertively, unconcerned who knows they are upset. Others are more careful and will try to mask their emotions, often without much success, until they explode, and we wonder, "Where did that come from?" because we missed the less obvious body language indicators. You may see people who are so angry they can't talk, or they can only talk through their clenched teeth, or their fists are balled up, or their faces are red, and they're just trying to hold themselves together. That person does not need a hug or a warning to "calm down." We need to use careful tones, create enough space and distance, and avoid triggering them with a condescending tone, dismissive body language, or the wrong words. You have to recognize those warning signs early, as do your coworkers. I've seen service situations where the employee will ask others later, "Was that person mad at me?" and the answer was a resounding yes.

We can look at their desire to avoid shame or embarrassment as two drivers of people and their behavior. We all feel this way; no one wants to be humiliated in public. Library staffers can do this accidentally or intentionally, just based on not reading the situation and the context accurately. When you announce in loud tones, to a patron trying to pay a book fine or a fee for his kid's reading program, in front of the whole world, "Sir, your credit card bounced and it didn't go through. You'll have to come up with another valid form of payment," that person will remember being shamed and embarrassed like that only for the next one hundred years. If it has happened to you, and you were embarrassed or shamed by a service provider, you can remember every detail of the encounter.

"But Steve, I was only doing my job! His card did bounce and I needed to collect his money in some other way." True and not true. You need to do your job with some tact, discretion, and empathy for his financial plight. It calls for a two-step process I call Physical Movement and the Assertive Whisper. With Physical Movement, you quietly ask the patron to step over to another part of your counter or desk: "Could I talk to you for a moment over here?" as you gesture toward a more private location, out of earshot of any others standing nearby. When the patron steps away with you, it's time for Step 2, the Assertive Whisper, which means to lower your voice to a near-whisper and tell him the facts: "I'm sorry to say your card didn't go through. Do you have another form of payment, or cash, or can you come back tomorrow with another way to pay?"

I believe in looking for ways to have careful, quiet, respectful, off-to-the-side conversations with patrons about certain things instead of having them in front of their kids, spouse, partner, friends, strangers, or other employees. If you don't and they get embarrassed, it really magnifies the intensity of the situation. You want to give the patron some face-saving options in a way that's sensitive to the fact that they don't want to be embarrassed in front of others around them.

SUPPORTING OUR BOSSES BEFORE A CRUCIAL CONVERSATION

Two communication concepts I discuss in my trainings relate to "alignment" and "changing the ratios of confrontation." The first says that sometimes you're the best person to talk to an angry, impatient patron, and other times it's better to have your coworker or boss take over because they are a better fit. Good alignment with another person is often based on the person "seeing himself or herself in the mirror" when talking with you. This could be based on being the same age, race, gender, sexual orientation, or even more likely, from being successful in a past encounter, where the patron felt well served by you. Perhaps you even developed a bit of a rapport during your discussion. In other words, they liked you enough to do business with you, and you solved their requests successfully.

Negative alignment is the opposite, where the patron won't talk to you or your colleague because there is no connection or there was a previous bad experience. In these instances, they may say, "I want to speak to your boss!" It's possible your boss comes over and says the exact same things you or your colleague just did and—It's a miracle!—the patron agrees or complies. (I hope you have the type of kind boss who will say, "I bet you said the same thing to him or her that I just did. Isn't it funny how he or she had to hear it from me?")

Having your boss or a coworker come over to support your efforts with the patron is called "changing the ratios of confrontation." Sometimes either or both your boss or a coworker will come over and actively help your discussion; other times one or both may just watch quietly from a distance, as a way to show their support but without stepping on your authority with the patron. Either way, it's a good strategy to use.

But we can mess up both the alignment and "change the ratios" tools by ambushing our boss during a difficult patron encounter. Imagine a scene where your boss is eating her lunch at her desk and going over e-mails when you come bursting through the door, saying "Come quick! There's an angry patron out here, and he wants to talk to you right away!"

With no preparation, no knowledge of the issue, and no backstory on the patron's complaint, your boss walks into a tough spot. This suggests two better alternatives: either tell the patron your boss is not available and handle it with your usual skill, patience, and professionalism, or tell the patron you are only allowed by policy to set an appointment with your boss, either by phone later today or in person tomorrow. This buys you some time to explain the situation to your boss, and it buys your boss some time to prepare for the conversation, either later today on the phone or tomorrow face to face. This may seem like we're passing the buck or needlessly delaying an inevitable encounter. Why not just solve it now, instead of waiting?

Lots of times what we discover is patrons leave or go home and forget about it or realize they got angry over nothing. If they decide to call back or come back, after the passage of two or twenty-four hours, they tend to be much more in control of their emotions. The anger and the intensity of the situation might have ebbed to the point where they can actually be reasonable in their conversation with the director, manager, or supervisor.

A similar approach would be to suggest to certain furious patrons—who, you suspect, will turn the phone call or the next-day meeting into a screamfest—that they must first reach out to your boss via e-mail. This is not a perfect solution, as some patrons can write ten-page, single-spaced, rambling, disconnected, fire-and-brimstone e-mails. For me, I would rather have them rant on paper than on the phone or to my face. Being told to only contact a supervisor by e-mail may infuriate an already angry patron, but then again, they may go home and not write a word, or if they do, we can interpret their words without having to hear the raised volume.

See if you can build to the approach of always setting phone, e-mail, or delayed appointments in your library, as a way to keep the emotional temperature down and give you and your boss more time to discuss the issue and prepare for the meeting.

SOME COMMUNICATION AND CONVERSATIONAL FINE POINTS

One of the conversational habits I think we all need to break is when we use the phrase, "yes, but" instead of "yes, and." Note how the word "but" is always followed by a disagreeing clause. Someone says to you, "I agree with you on Issue X, but . . ."; the very next thing they say will be a complete disagreement with your take on Issue X. Whenever someone says, "I'm not going to say you're wrong, but . . ." the next words are about how wrong he or she thinks you are. Whatever you said they will flip around and minimize. Anything that comes before the "but" gets crossed out after the "but." It's a simple and more positive semantic shift to say "and" instead of "but." "I agree with what you said and I have a perspective that suggests this . . ." or "I hear what you're saying and I'd like to talk about this other point here" or "I agree with what you're saying, and here are some other things about this issue." So whenever someone says "I hate to disagree with you, but . . ." you know that they're going to disagree with you. You can make a small but important shift from "but" to "and." I try to use "and" as much as I can in conversations, but I don't always succeed.

In his *Verbal Judo* book, George Thompson discussed the value of using a more formal discussion process with angry people. This can help you assert your authority without being too officious about it.

Let's say an angry patron is shouting at one of your coworkers or you're a supervisor and they're shouting at one of your staff; try this approach:

"Good afternoon, sir. I'm Steve from the library here. I'm the assistant manager (or the children's librarian, or whatever your title happens to be). Is it okay if we talk for a moment?"

If the patron agrees or doesn't agree, keep going.

"Okay, thanks. The reason I came over was it looks like you might need some help that I may be able to provide for you. Or it looks like there are some things here that I may be able to do for you, once you tell me what you need, or once you tell me what you're looking to do. My colleague and I may be able to help you. Can I get you to do that for me?"

Let's look at the structure of this conversation. The first thing you do is come over and greet this person: good afternoon, good morning, good evening. The second thing is you've identified yourself as having a title and it's not a superiority thing; it just says "I want you to see me as a professional here in the library environment, so here's what I do here." The third thing is you explained the reason you came over. The real reason you came over was to help out and support your colleague. You're saying to this person, "I'm not going to allow this conversation to escalate. I want you to tell me your story."

Continuing, you can ask questions that ask the person to justify his behavior.

"What's making you so upset? Did we do something that made you angry? Did you have a problem with somebody else before I got here? Because you sound upset to me. Is there something that we did or something happened that made you upset?"

Sometimes the person will justify his behavior and go off on an angry tangent. But what you're trying to do in this situation is at least plant a seed that says, "Your behavior is inappropriate here. You're a bit out of control. When the person has to explain it, he may realize—grudgingly—it's not really that big a deal, and maybe he kind of overstepped.

At that point, you can request more cooperation:

"Could I ask you to come with me over here? Could I ask you to step over to the desk with me? Could you come with me over to this computer terminal while I take a quick look? Could I ask you to wait right here at this chair and just grab a quick seat here until I return from the back office? Will you do that for me?"

You request their cooperation, and with that, you can see if he is a "Yes," "Maybe," or "No" person, and do what you can do to solve the issue, get even more information, or clarify what you will do or solve, and close the conversation.

"Okay, were you looking for this book? Were you looking for that website? Is this the answer you need?"

And if that solves the problem then thank him for his patience. What's that, you say? This guy wasn't patient at all; he was rude, abrupt, and obnoxious. Okay, I'll agree. Thank him for his patience anyway.

We're trying to "coach up" this patron a bit, by demonstrating professional communication tools to a person who may not even recognize what those are. We're trying to model what appropriate adults do in the library environment.

"Thanks for coming in. Thanks for your patience. Thanks for your cooperation. I hope I was or we were able to help."

Those are good closure statements to get this person on his way.

Let's talk about the value of humor in certain situations that can be high-stress communication situations. You're not doing a standup comedy routine, and I get it. And sometimes jokes can be inappropriate and wrong for the seriousness of the situation. You've seen people make dumb jokes in serious meetings, and things like that throw people off track. What I'm talking about sometimes is self-deprecating humor, a lighter touch, that seeks to humanize you. "I hate these computer systems sometimes, don't you? They're supposed to make our lives easier but they can make my life tougher, you know? If I have to change my password to my other dog's name one more time, I'm going to go crazy, right?"

It can give the other person a sense that you're a human being too, struggling with the same issues that we're all struggling with. A little humor, never aimed at them or anybody else, but always just poking fun at yourself sort of puts them and you on an even keel. It says we're all in this together.

THE CODE OF QUALITY SERVICE FOR LIBRARY EMPLOYEES

In 1985, my father, Dr. Karl Albrecht, wrote *Service America! Doing Business in the New Economy*,[4] the first big book on customer service. He described service excellence as a "managed event," meaning it was something that business leaders, managers, and supervisors should carefully consider and focus on with their employees. "Good service is no accident," was a primary theme of his book. He talked about having the right three things in place: Service Strategies (the direction), Service Systems (the methods, approaches, and policies), and Service People (the right employees, with the right attitude, training, and motivation to serve others). He referred to this as the Service Triangle™, and it still works today.

Part of his efforts to train frontline service employees was to create the Code of Quality Service, a set of ten behaviors that can provide a path to service excellence, both personally and professionally.

This set of ten can be useful as a reminder for you as a library service professional and as a set of training guidelines for managers and supervisors. It works as a refresher for longtime library employees and as an orientation tool for new employees, as to what our library service culture should look like. Most of these ten are operational and not abstract, meaning you can put them to use right away.

1. *Greet each patron immediately or when passing by.*
   This concept is about both politeness and safety. We want to see patrons as they enter the library and pay attention to them as they move through the facility. Respectful eye contact can help us all make a human connection. We can all benefit from looking more at people and less at screens.

2. *Give each patron you contact your complete attention.*
   It's easy to get caught up or distracted by the work we need to do. What we call "multitasking" on the patrons' behalf is actually "split attention" or "being distracted." It's a simple step just to tell patrons, anytime you need to do a part of your job that requires you to disengage from them. "I'll just need a quick moment to step over to the computer and take a look at your record" or "Let me go and ask one of my coworkers about that and I'll come right back to you." Those types of statements are enough to buy you the time to do your job and serve them well.

3. *Make the first thirty seconds count.*
   This concept is related to number 9 as well. Patrons remember how they were treated by recalling the beginning and the end of the service encounter. You may have only a brief interaction with a patron, but he or she will remember your approachability, tone, and helpfulness.

4. *Play your part to be real, not phony or bored.*
   If you have a high-human-contact job, with a lot of the same transactions that don't require a lot of creativity to get them done, it's easy to get tired, burned out, and become what Karl calls a "BoZo" or a "Bored Zombie." Change what you say and how you say it with each patron. Don't get robotic in your answers, greetings, or wrap-ups. We've all dealt with service people who say, "Have a nice day—NEXT!" and don't really mean it.

5. *Show your energy with sincere friendliness.*
   Whether you're talking over the phone, over the counter, or in the stacks, know that you're being viewed as a representative of the library. Patrons don't care about job titles or how long you've been there; they want service from someone who is truly friendly, not faking it, and who has the type of enthusiasm that says they care about their jobs and about helping people, at the start of the workday and the end of it.

6. *Be the patron's problem solver.*
   Own the patron's issue until you can solve it or get it over to a colleague or boss who can. This step is all about not brushing off our patrons, but

taking ownership for that brief moment or long period when you're helping them. Be creative, within the limits of our policies, and solve the presenting problem the best way you can, the first time.

7. *Use your common sense.*

    We've all been in service situations where the person on the other side of the counter or on the other end of the phone has not been authorized to think. This person could come up with a smart solution but just won't. You get paid to think and work on behalf of our patrons. Do the right thing for them, using a common-sense sensibility.

8. *Bend the rules when the situation calls for it.*

    Don't give away the store, but if you can solve the patron's problem or fix the issue by using creative, empathic solutions, do so. If you can waive a fee or a fine and it makes sense, get permission from your boss and do it. Don't always get stuck in the fine print of the policy manual or the Code of Conduct. Don't say to the patron, "Well, I'm just doing my job by saying no to you." Know the difference between the "letter of the law" and the "spirit of the law." Like with number 6, be the patron's advocate if you can.

9. *Make the last thirty seconds count.*

    Like with number 3, the end of your service encounter with patrons can make a big difference in how they see their library experience. Thank your patrons for coming in, or for being patient while you worked on their behalf. Even if they don't thank you back, thank them anyway.

10. *Take good care of yourself.*

    Service jobs are challenging and tiring. Don't get burned out. Take your breaks and lunches, and use your vacation days and floating holidays. Pace yourself throughout your workday. Get more sleep, get some exercise, and catch up on your reading or other hobbies as a way to stay fresh and focused. Help yourself have a long and healthy career in library service.

Karl Albrecht's Code of Quality Service offers ten easy and practical steps toward improving and sustaining your own brand of service excellence.

NOTES

1. https://www.ala.org/pla/sites/ala.org.pla/files/content/data/PLA_Staff_Survey_Report_2022.pdf. Page 6.
2. Joseph Grenny, Kerry Patterson, Al Switzler, and Ron McMillan, *Crucial Conversations: Tools for Talking When Stakes Are High* (New York: McGraw-Hill, 2002).
3. George Thompson, *Verbal Judo: The Gentle Art of Persuasion* (New York: William Morrow, 1993; updated 2013).
4. Karl Albrecht and Ron Zemke, *Service America! Doing Business in the New Economy* (Homewood, IL: Dow Jones-Irwin, 1985).

2

Training Library Staff in Service, Safety, and Security

FOCUS ON THE NEED PREMISE

We send employees to training classes—live or on Zoom—to help them change or improve their work performance, to change their thinking as to how to handle service issues, and help them improve their behavior (if necessary) with colleagues and bosses.

We send directors, managers, and supervisors to training to help them add to the tools in their respective tool kits. We want them to be able to leverage their time, experience, and influence and address employee behavior and performance issues with coaching skills and patron issues with leadership experience and service skills.

We want both sets of participants to take what they need from the learning sessions and begin to apply the ideas to a better library. Sounds easy, right? Well, it's not. Training is not a cure-all or a miracle fix, nor should it be seen as a "check the box" day, where we "round up the usual suspects" and dump some knowledge on them. It had better have a purpose, meaning, and practical use or it's a waste of everyone's time (including the trainer's time and energy, as I can well attest, having taught sessions no one wanted to be at, for subjects management thought the staff needed, but didn't).

As I look around the library training landscape right now, specifically for subjects that I know well, several themes appear. (I would define these as Tough Training Topics.) See if some of these library-specific training issues might just resonate with you and your colleagues:

Service burnout. Library employees start calling in sick with an "I" problem, as in, "I don't want to come in today. I'm sick of these patrons and this place. I can't do this anymore. I need to make a change to my work and life." I would argue that 50 percent of job burnout is on the shoulders of the employee. They need to discover what is burning them out and make changes. The other 50 percent is the responsibility of their bosses—to make changes, to provide new opportunities, and to make their jobs more interesting and rewarding—and worthy of doing well again.

Compassion fatigue. It gets tiring being exposed to patrons who have a lot of hard life issues, many of which we cannot solve easily or ever. It's hard to be empathic, positive, and patient every single day.

Trauma exposure. It's tough to be exposed to other people's trauma, which can become triggering for our own histories as well. Library staff may see people who are in pain, angry, hostile, demanding, suffering from depression, or living with hidden or visible disabilities, and who have been mistreated or are mistreating others. It adds up.

Countertransference concerns. We care too much about our patrons, and then after we get burned out or disillusioned about them or our career, we don't care about them as much as we should. Therapists, cops, firefighters, paramedics, and medical professionals face the same issues in their work, and it can create a crossroads decision point for them.

Harassment prevention. "Leave me alone! Let me do my job! Don't say or do those things around me!" Unlike the private sector or in male-dominated workplaces, library harassment comes mostly from patrons and not from co-workers or bosses. The usual training need for this subject shifts when it's our customers who are the primary problem. All of the next chapter is devoted to this concerning issue.

Security training. How will staff handle patron behavioral issues, security problems, and safety hazards? Can we educate them on high-risk (active shooter) and low-risk (noisy patron) events, so they feel empowered to handle both? Can we train them to develop best practices they all share and do, consistently, accurately, and with empathy?

New-employee orientation. How do we onboard people into our facility, define the work culture for our library, and orient them as to our service goals? How do we help them understand the need for personal and professional vigilance, to keep them and their patrons safe?

Existing employee motivation. What gets your employees out of bed each morning to come to work? It's more than just the reward of the paycheck. We know people will donate their time and energy for free—at their kid's school, for their church, for a civic group or community organization—because it feels good. How do we motivate staff to continue to do a job that can be tough and filled with daily conflicts, requiring them to be on their feet and all-knowing, all day?

Coaching skills for library leaders, managers, and supervisors. Good bosses coach, every day. They give feedback, not criticism, to their employees. They give praise when it's deserved and support all the time. They coach for better performance and better behaviors, using *lots of opportunities to model and explain what they want.*

START WITH ASSESSMENTS, SURVEYS, QUESTIONS, AND OBSERVATIONS

Management guru Tom Peters is most famous for a bestselling business book he wrote in 1982 with Bob Waterman called *In Search of Excellence.*[1] Peters is also known for a clever concept he coined called "MBWA" or "Management By Walking Around" (and also widely called "Management By Wandering Around," which I like better because it sounds more fun). He meant that good bosses get out of their offices and watch things, observe interactions with staff and customers, listen more than talk, and pay careful and sometimes quiet attention to how their people do their work and the challenges they face while doing it. Besides just moving around the facility, library leaders will need to work from collected data, not just guesswork. What seems like it is or is not an issue needs verification.

Consider these data-gathering tools for library leaders to make good decisions about what kinds of training staff needs, taught by whom (outside consultants or inside subject-matter experts), when, where, and via what format (online, Zoom, small-group, one-on-one coaching, or all-staff sessions):

Annual Employee Quality of Worklife (EQWL) surveys: This written or online survey document asks employees a lot about what it's like to work at the library: how they perceive they are treated; the apparent work culture; their opportunities to improve or advance; the management style of their supervisors, managers, and leaders; and what needs to be improved, left alone, or eliminated in their workplace.

Regular patron feedback / customer satisfaction surveys: These can be done online or via comment cards, focus group interviews, or community meetings. It's useful to know what your customers really want versus what we think they want.

Complete policy and operations manual reviews: Using a stem-to-stern approach, it can be useful to do a thorough review of our new-employee orientation materials, employee handbooks, HR-related policies and procedures, and safety and security protocols. Some of these need to be edited down, tightened up, eliminated, rewritten completely, or improved, based on new legal or HR laws.

Meetings with internal/external experts: Whether it's outside consultants who are skilled in specific or general library subjects, or our own in-house training experts, it's good to know who we know, who we have, and what they can do for us.

Departmental inventory, safety, and security audits: These are sometimes referred to as "Inspection and Control Audits." (I've provided an example of one in appendix B.) It tells us what we have, what we need to buy or replace, and what we need to better protect: employees, patrons, our facility, our physical assets, our physical and electronic financial instruments, our IT system, and such.

This search for data, library system-wide certainly results in reports, potential solutions, the need for deadlines, and necessary changes. All these will be managed around what I always call the Big Three: the costs (Can we afford it, now or later?), the work culture (Is it a good fit? Will it make our culture stronger?), and the feasibility (Can we do it and how?).

STOP APOLOGIZING FOR THE NEED FOR SECURITY

Think about all the security devices in your world. I have a Subaru Outback. I love my car, mostly, especially in the snow. Every time I press the unlock button on my key ring, it unlocks the driver's side door, which is great, but I always forget to press it the second time or sometimes the third or fourth time, so it will unlock the back passenger door. I curse under my breath that I can't remember how to operate my own car. I've owned the beast for seven years.

When I lived in California, I had a sliding glass door that I put a big stick into the frame to keep it locked, in case somebody tried to pry it open. Every morning, I would go to let my forty-three (or so it seems like I have) dogs out, unlock the door lock, try to pull it open, and forget the stick was in there. I would then have to bend down and pick it up and let them out. How could I forget the stick was there, every morning? Same cursing under my breath as with the Outback door.

Then it struck me: stop apologizing for having security. And it's the same thing I'd like to tell you, doing whatever job you do in the library: stop apologizing for library security. I know it's a hassle to use your hard key or key card to get into the staff entrance. I know it's stressful to remember the burglar alarm code when you open up on a Saturday morning and you have twelve seconds to enter it before the system calls the cops. I know it's tedious to type your user name and password into the computer system. I get it, better than most, since it's the world I've known since I was twenty-one.

When you think about the things that you have in place already at the library for security, there are lots of things that we probably take for granted. You have exterior lights around the building and in the parking lot. You have interior lights in the hallways and stairwells and around areas of the library where it's dark. You may have convex mirrors up in the ceiling corners so you can see into the corners. You may have camera systems that cover the outside and inside of the building, and that cover the parking lot, even at night. Those cameras probably record to a digital video recorder (DVR) or network video recorder (NVR), so you or your boss or the cops can look at it later. We have security for our IT systems, Wi-Fi protections, firewalls, and passwords for our servers. Our IT specialists have all kinds of software and hardware and all kinds of barriers they put in place to keep our systems from being hacked and compromised by ransomware.

Some libraries use radio frequency identification (RFID) tags on books, DVDs, and other high-theft materials. Some libraries have panic alarms under the desks, at the Circulation, Reference, or Information desks, and even in the back office. Some libraries may even have personal panic alarms that staff have on a lanyard as they walk the library floor. You may have security guards stationed in your library, all the time, only on weekends or at night, or after school gets out. There are a lot of interior, exterior, invisible, obvious, and not-so-obvious security devices in libraries already.

You may have library pages or specific employees who serve in a security function. This could be a retired law enforcement person, or people who were in the military and who want to help out the library. We have the police in some libraries, especially in downtown branches, who are assigned there full time or part time, who work there as part of the city police or county sheriff's contract. We have door locks opened by hard keys or electronic key cards. (I'm a big fan of key cards because if an employee loses them or quits, we can make the switch and get them a new one, or take them out of the system instantaneously. If employees lose hard keys to the library, sometimes they won't tell us for weeks on end because they're embarrassed, they don't want to get into any trouble, and now we have a set of keys to the facility floating around out there.)

We have access control policies for our buildings, during and after hours. We have burglar alarms, fire alarms, and locked storage facilities in larger libraries where there's a warehouse where books and other materials are delivered. We have warehouse storage cages, where we can lock up certain theft-sensitive items like laptops, tablets, PCs, printer toner, and other items that can be stolen.

We have security policies and procedures for emergency evacuations, active shooters, trespassing, and behavior issues that are connected to our Codes of Conduct. We don't need to apologize for asking all employees to wear visible ID badges.

We have (or should have) vigilance behavior by our staff, supervisors, PICs (persons in charge), managers, and directors. We may even have vigilance behavior by our patrons, who might report things that happen related to safety and security. "Hey, some kids are fighting outside! A guy is sleeping in the bathroom. There are some people over here doing this and that." We have Security Incident Reports (SIRs), which can give us information about safety or security hazards, devices, equipment, or parts of the facility that are broken and need to be fixed, or are potential hazards to a child, a disabled person, or a patron who could get injured walking by it or into it. All those things are usually quite common in the library world.

So if we look at all the things that exist in the library for security, it includes policies, procedures, response protocols, equipment, devices, and an employee and management culture to keep us, the patrons, the collection materials, and the facility safe. We shouldn't have to apologize, rationalize, explain, or make excuses as to why we have these things in place, either to each other (which we sometimes do), to our elected officials, to our patrons, or to anyone we are there to protect. We shouldn't have to apologize for security improvements within our library that exist now or could in the future. We shouldn't have to apologize for asking patrons to comply with our Code of Conduct. We shouldn't have had to apologize for asking people to comply with the COVID-19 rules during the eras of masks and social distancing.

No need to apologize for having visitor and vendor policies, or a structured system in place for how we manage visitors who want to go into the back offices and see an employee or the library director, or vendors who need to make deliveries or repairs.

People who are coming in for legitimate reasons, or who have an appointment and want to speak to a library director or supervisor about a bona fide issue, should not complain if we do some screening to figure out what their issues are. We should not allow angry people to go storming into our back offices, especially where our leadership team works. We shouldn't have to apologize for having a visitor screening process. There should be no exceptions, even for vendors or delivery people who need to sign in to get into the back of our facility.

As you'll see with an example in appendix E, I think it's critically important to have an event plan for every public or private event that we have with twenty-five or more people. We should not apologize for having a security plan that addresses those things that might never happen but could happen. We have an author coming in for a book signing. We have a group of kids coming in from the local elementary school to watch a play. We have seniors coming in for a musical performance. We will need a plan for how we protect those people inside our building; in our auditoriums and theaters; on our plazas, patios, and courtyards; or in our training rooms.

We should not apologize for thinking in advance about events that may have never happened before, might not ever happen, or probably wouldn't happen. The past is not a good predictor of the future but it gives us indicators, does it not? In this current age, with protests, demonstrations, or even riots happening in and around public buildings, we have a duty to think about the worst-case scenario when it comes to protecting people who are coming into our facility or for a group event. Maybe it's a nighttime event, maybe it's a group size we've never had before, or maybe we've had lots of experience and practice with handling large groups. Either way, we need to look continually at how we bring people in and out in a safe way.

CREATING A "CHALLENGE CULTURE" IN THE LIBRARY

So instead of apologizing for our safety and security procedures, instead of apologizing for security equipment, we should be continuing to create and establish and reward what is called a "challenge culture." A challenge culture says our employees feel comfortable and empowered by us to challenge people who are not following or violating our security procedures, whether it's a patron or a vendor trying to get in through the back doors of the library without permission.

Our employees don't have to be quasi-security guards, but we want them to embrace the idea that they're just as responsible and just as "in charge of security" (and safety and service quality) as anybody else. They can and should see things and notify each other, our leaders, or the police (without having to ask permission to call 9-1-1) and recognize potential or actual problems before the senior staff does.

I'm always in favor of praising employees who point out what we need to fix—whether it's a safety hazard, a security failure, a lighting issue on the stairway, something that's wet or broken, an electrical hazard, a slippery floor, or some kind of spilled or leaked hazmat—way before anybody from facilities, maintenance, or the janitorial staff would see it.

I have done site security assessments in libraries and said, "You have twelve cameras in this system and only eight of them work. What's wrong with the other four cameras?" And the staff will say, "Those have been broken for years." I say, "Who is responsible for fixing the cameras?"

"Well, we told management about it, but they didn't do anything to get them fixed, so we just live with it." Wrong answer.

The message here becomes, "Don't bother to say anything to our bosses about what needs to be fixed or repaired because they just won't do anything." I'm not saying you have to fix everything as soon as it comes to your attention—unless it's a hazard or it's dangerous. Some security-related repairs, upgrades, or improvements need a requisition, repair order, or purchase order. But sometimes the message to our employees is it doesn't matter if you tell us about things that need to be fixed if we just can't get to it or we're not going to bother to tell you when we are going to get to it. What the employees hear is, "My input about security is not important or valid." That's not the challenge culture that we want.

In my Perfect Library World, I would give employees rewards, like Amazon, Starbucks, or gas station cards every time they pointed out something significant that's broken, needs repair, or is a safety hazard. If we didn't recognize it and they saw it way before we did, that's worth rewarding. Employees follow our lead on this issue, and the message from the leadership team should be "every security failure, security equipment issue, or patron behavioral concern is a concern to us all, not just to the leadership team, or the police, or the security guards, but everybody. We're all in charge of safety and security."

We shouldn't apologize for asking our in-house or contract security guard to do his or her job more effectively, more courteously, or more safely. We shouldn't have staff apologizing to the library leadership for calling 9-1-1 if that's what they felt they needed to do. As I say in my training programs, if your intuition says to call the police, then call the police. Explain to us why afterward. You can't call the police if somebody looks at you funny but you don't have to wait to be assaulted or for something violent to happen before you call the police. We should use the police as a force multiplier in those situations where someone is armed, wants to hurt people, or is threatening to hurt himself or others. If we create a culture where employees feel embarrassed to call 9-1-1 or that they shouldn't call 9-1-1 without permission, that could turn into a tragedy. We need to praise employees when they use good judgment, communication and service tools, and intuition.

Sometimes I see library supervisors and managers apologize to their maintenance, facilities, or janitorial staff when they've asked them to clean up or fix something. That's their job. We should ask them courteously but we shouldn't apologize for having them come in and do the things we need them to do, like replace lights, fix a camera system, or clean up a serious spill. We would have that same conversation if we brought in an outside vendor. We should appreciate what they do, praise them when it's done well, and thank them, but we shouldn't apologize for asking them to work.

I don't think we should be apologizing to city managers and county administrative officers, council members, board of supervisors, elected or appointed officials, or library board members when we ask for budget dollars to make security or safety improvements. There's a perception we have to go hat in hand for budget dollars for things that just make good common sense when it comes to security. We aren't being frivolous with the taxpayer's money; we're making an investment in keeping patrons and staff safe. We're making an investment to limit our future liability. We're making an investment in our security that says to any plaintiff's attorneys that we're taking care of our people.

And stop apologizing to patrons for what they might perceive as "security inconveniences." Stop saying, "Sorry, we had to have you go through the book alarm. Sorry, you couldn't get in this area; this is for staff only." Stop apologizing for things that we should be doing as part of our regular way of keeping the library safe.

My standard speech to patrons would be, "You know, there are the things that we have to do in our world now, to keep everybody safe, including you and your kids, and whoever else comes in here. Even though it might not seem like it at the time, we're doing this for good reasons. We have discussions about our security procedures and we'll continue to talk about what we need to do and improve. If you have some suggestions, let us know. We want to teach our new employees, our new hires as part of new employee orientation, that this is a security culture. We enjoy our work, we're supportive of everybody here, and we offer good service to everybody that comes in here. But we have a security mind-set as well, and part of our job duties, besides good customer service, is paying attention to the patron safety and library behavioral concerns."

I think about patron behavior as part of my work as a library security consultant and about not having to apologize when we ban a patron for high-risk behavior that consistently violates our Code of Conduct or our policies. Issues like sexual or racial harassment, threatening our staff or other patrons, inappropriate touching, or harming other people in the library means it's time for consequences, not apologies. For example, "Sorry we have to do this, but . . ."

We should not be sorry; the patrons drove us to this result with their behavior; we didn't just pick them randomly out of the crowd.

Sometimes we need to give patrons second and third chances to get their act together and get their behavior under control, and sometimes we just need to say this person is not allowed in our facility, not allowed in our library, after even one event. When it comes to clients being injured based on the actions of another person, like a patron who intentionally injures another patron by starting a fight, the plaintiff's attorneys are always looking at foreseeability and prior notice. Foreseeability says could we have predicted this might happen or would happen, based on this person's behavior in the past. Prior notice means do we have documented incidents about this person's behavior, that we knew about it, it has happened, or it's been going on for a while, and now it happened again. With foreseeability and prior notice, we don't have to predict the future, but we do have to look at things that have happened once with the possibility that they may happen again and that's not ever what we want.

So when it comes to patron behavior that is high risk or dangerous—for example, harassment, bullying, inappropriate touching, threats, fighting, indecent exposure, or stealing—we need to say there is a line in the sand that we draw about problematic behavior that violates either the law or our Code of Conduct. There are no exceptions and no second, third, or fourth chances.

We should not allow any type of patron—whether it's teenagers, predatory homeless people, out-of-control mentally ill people, people on drugs or under the influence of alcohol—to come in and take over our building and make our citizens feel afraid to come to the library or stay there. We should not apologize for enforcing our rules for that small number of people that can be problematic, to the point where people don't want to go to the library, drop off their kids, or allow their teenagers to study there. If regular people from our community are afraid to use the library, they will tell others, especially using social media, and we will put ourselves at the bottom of a long hill to climb back up to a reasonable, safe facility.

I feel strongly that we should feel empowered about our facilities. We should feel empowered about protecting our staff and the patrons who come in. We shouldn't apologize for the things that we need to do.

USING SCENARIOS AND ROLE-PLAYS DURING STAFF MEETINGS

In my Perfect Library World, staff members would gather on an irregular, as-needed basis to create, discuss, and select their best conversational and interventional solutions to the most challenging patron interactions they face. After all, they are the ones who have to deal with these situations, so why not have them create the best responses, getting the blessings from their supervisors and managers, too? Using role-plays, where they break into small groups (no need to make it stressful, "performing" in front of colleagues), they can work through several scenarios, playing the parts of the Challenging Patron or the

(Perhaps Confused, Thinking Fast) Employee. The goal for their work through the scenarios is to share their best practices, the approaches that seem to work best, with their coworkers.

The following scenarios are based on real events given to me by real librarians. There are no easy or perfect answers. Each scene will take some work by the employee playing the part of the Library Employee. It's always easier to play the role of the Challenging Patron because you can veer off in any kind of odd or erratic direction that you want to, as your colleague gamely tries to keep you within the bounds of the scripted scenario. Try not to be too rough on your coworkers. As they start to get you back into line, comply. The goal for these high-stress, no-perfect-answer scenarios is empowerment, not tears; success, not frustration. The group can fine-tune what they saw as successful, get a thumbs up from the bosses, and go forth and use these when and if these situations arise.

Consider these situations as more than just Usual Patron Stuff and more like Unusual Patron Stuff. (I have provided a few jumping-off discussion points for you and your colleagues to consider.)

SCENARIO 1

A patron is spanking his child, quite hard. The child is in tears, the man seems very angry, and other patrons and staff are concerned.

(Call the police? Wait until he leaves and call Child Protective Services [CPS]? Intervene, with several colleagues? Call him out, publicly, to stop?)

SCENARIO 2

An elderly patron in a wheelchair is brought into the library by someone who appears to be her caregiver. The caregiver wheels her up to a table and leaves her alone. Several hours later, the caregiver still has not returned, and the woman seems to be in distress. It's not clear if the caregiver is still even in the library.

(Page the caregiver? Check on the woman for possible medical problems or bathroom needs? Call Adult Protective Services [APS] if this happens repeatedly?)

SCENARIO 3

An adult woman is known by all library staff to be developmentally disabled. She is friendly and loves visiting the library. Lately, she has started hugging and kissing everyone she sees: staff members, startled patrons, and small children. It's uncomfortable for everyone. You have spoken to her caregiver, who says, "Oh, she's harmless. She's touchy-feely that way. No need to overreact about it. She just likes people."

(Better boundaries? Another conversation with the caregiver? Do we need to call APS for guidance? Call a social worker for an answer?)

SCENARIO 4

A man comes into the library holding a small plastic bucket and dressed in what appears to be priest's clothing (black shirt, white notched collar, black suit coat). He goes from table to table throughout the library, asking patrons for "donations to help the homeless." He has even asked staff members to contribute. When you tell him he cannot solicit money in the library, he says he is doing the "Lord's work" (and names a church and religious group you have never heard of). He says he will not stop because he is "on a mission from God."

(Is this a scam or legitimate? Is he showing signs of mental illness? Do you have a policy about soliciting in the library? Does he have the legal right to do this?)

SCENARIO 5

A female patron has accused another female patron of stealing her cell phone. A library security officer responds and asks the accused patron for permission to examine her purse and backpack. She complies and shows her own cell phone. The patron who made the accusation suddenly finds her own cell phone and is deeply embarrassed. The accused patron is furiously outraged and demands that you and the security officer "do something." She wants the other woman arrested for making a false accusation.

(Call the police? Ask the other woman to apologize? Explain that you can't do much? Tell the security officer to handle it?)

SCENARIO 6

A group of four people come into the library and start taking cell phone pictures of the facility, staff members, and patrons. One of the group sets up a tripod with a small video camera on it, right in front of the Circulation Desk. He starts filming people while his colleagues try to bait the staff and nearby patrons into a political discussion.

(Enforce our "no photos / no videos" policy, if we have one? Call the police? Have a manager ask them to leave? Ignore them?)

SCENARIO 7

An older male patron is seated at the internet computers. He is wearing his own headphones as he watches a movie on the screen. He starts passing gas, loudly and repetitively. The smell is pretty powerful. What seems sort of funny is now annoying other patrons. He seems oblivious as to what he is doing.

(Is this the first time, or has he done this before? Cognitive issues? Is he doing this on purpose or by accident?)

SCENARIO 8

A young adult keeps using a vape pen in the library. At first, it looks like it's emitting the usual vape-flavored fumes. But now it seems like you're getting a whiff of marijuana from it. This is not the first time you have warned him about this.

(What is the vaping policy? What are the pot laws in your state? Time for a short suspension?)

SCENARIO 9

A woman who appears to have mental health issues sits in the corner of the library making loud comments and cursing. Her language is racist, sexist, homophobic, and graphic toward people and various religions. When you confront her, she cites her "First Amendment Rights to Free Speech."

(Hate speech policy? Need for a social worker? Ask her to leave? Ban her?)

SCENARIO 10

A patron comes to you and says that as she and her daughter were walking by the internet use area when a man exposed himself to both of them. He is still sitting there. She says she doesn't want to get involved or call the police, but she wanted you to know what happened. She leaves. When you confront the male patron, he denies this behavior. As you talk, you see pornography on his personal tablet.

(Call the police? Check the video camera footage? Ask him to leave immediately?)

SCENARIO 11

A young man comes into your work area and asks you for the time. You tell him, and he nods and goes to sit at a nearby table. He doesn't have a book or anything else with him. He just sits and stares intently at you and the other female staffers and female patrons. This goes on for two hours. Staff and patrons are starting to feel uncomfortable and complain. When you ask him to stop staring, he nods, complies for a while, and then starts doing it again.

(Autism? Immaturity? Poor social skills? What is his intent? Ask him to leave?)

SCENARIO 12

A woman comes in and tells you she is living on the streets. She asks you if she can use the small restroom in your small library. You give her the key and she goes inside and you can hear her lock the door. An hour later, she is still in there. Other patrons are starting to complain they can't use the restroom because she won't come out.

(Medical problem? Call an ambulance if she won't answer? Drug or alcohol use? Sleeping in there? Tell her you will call the police if she doesn't leave? Open the door with your master key?)

NOTE

1. Tom Peters and Robert H. Waterman Jr., *In Search of Excellence: Lessons from America's Best-Run Companies* (New York: HarperCollins, 1982).

3

Preventing Harassment of Library Staff

RESPONDING TO SEXUAL OR RACIAL BEHAVIORS BY PATRONS

Before I begin my discussion of this challenging patron behavior issue, I'll offer a few words about my words. It's common to see the phrase "this employee was a victim of sexual or racial harassment in the workplace." I prefer to substitute the word "target" for the word "victim," and will do so throughout this chapter. To me, "victim" suggests an ongoing traumatization, which can become a label or even a yoke for the person who has experienced and reported the harassment. It makes better semantic sense for me to describe how library employees are "targets" of harassment because I think it's more empowering to say you no longer are a target of the patron and have stopped those negative encounters, on your own and/or with management support.

The issue of unreported sexual harassment of library staff members is a growing concern that has existed in the shadows for far too long. When I teach live programs at a library, it's quite common for a female employee to come up to me, look over her shoulder a few times, drop her voice to a near-whisper, and say, "Can I ask you a question about this guy who has bothered me at work?" Their stories are achingly common, and sometimes these behaviors have been going on unchecked for so long that the employee is ready to quit. If that happens, that is a failure on the part of management not doing its collective job.

While sexual harassment is certainly possible for same-sex sexual orientation or when it's aimed at male employees, the majority of these cases involve female employees being harassed by male patrons. Most of these behaviors start as unwanted flirting, prying personal questions, or inappropriate attempts at physical contact (hugging, blocking, staring, coming too close, following). Left unaddressed and with no consequences for the patron's behavior, the harassment escalates, including bothering the staff member outside of work, or even stalking her.

These comments and language often come from certain (usually male) patrons toward library staff (often female, but this happens to male employees and LGBTQ employees as well.) It's a concern I've seen as I've traveled to libraries around the country. When they are put on notice about this issue, library leaders must intervene to increase the peace of mind of their staff, stop these comments or behaviors, and enhance the safety of all library employees.

When female employees tell me these stories and I ask if they have told their direct supervisors, or the library director, I hear answers like these: "I didn't want to bother my boss with this; I just want it to stop." Or, "I was afraid to tell my supervisor because I didn't want her/him to think it was my fault for not stopping it sooner." Or, "I didn't want to be blamed for the patron's behavior." Or, "I wasn't sure who to tell. My direct supervisor? HR? The director?"

Worse yet, I've also heard this collection of horrible responses from supervisors to employees who report inappropriate patron behavior to their bosses: "My supervisor told me I should be 'flattered by the attention.'" "My boss told me the patron was 'mostly harmless' and that I shouldn't worry about him, and that he does that with everybody. He's just joking or kidding around." "He does that with all the girls here, even other patrons. He's just eccentric." "He's a pain, but he's also a very important member of our community." "Well, you told him to stop once. I'm not sure what else I can do." None of these excuses or rationalizations are valid, and they demean the reporting process.

There are several disturbing issues here: a noticeable "Blame the target/shoot the messenger" mentality; a lack of response by managers and supervisors who should know better, based on their training and experience with this important workplace issue; and a desire to ignore a set of behaviors that often escalates. This issue needs an enforced policy, better boundaries for patrons, support for employee-targets, and consequences for patron-perpetrators.

The response by library supervisors, managers, and directors should be, when an employee comes to their office, "Come in, let's sit down, let's talk about what happened here, let me close the door, and let's have a private conversation about this specific situation, with examples, so I can work with you to figure what we will do about it."

Sexual and racial harassment was made illegal by the passage of the Civil Rights Act in 1964, signed by President Johnson. Of course policies and legislation don't stop actual behaviors, but it certainly gives us consequences to enforce and we know that these illegal behaviors are what get organizations into problems if they don't step up and protect their employees from these types of things.

Sexual or racial harassment prevention will always require management vigilance, multiple channels of reporting, an investigative process, updated policies that support targeted employees and punish patron-perpetrators, and the necessary courage for all employees to report if they are harassed or even witness other employees being harassed.

We also need to tell all bystander library employees, "Just because it's not happening directly to you doesn't make it acceptable behavior. If you were a bystander or a witness to sexually or racially harassing behaviors by a patron, you need to have the courage to tell our directors, managers, supervisors, Human Resources (HR), or the agency's attorney what you have seen, overheard, or were told by other targeted employees, who may be too afraid of retaliation to report it themselves."

Retaliation, which is illegal and unethical in all our workplaces, takes on many forms. Some targeted employees are retaliated against by coworkers when they report harassment, some by management, and some by the patron-perpetrators. "How dare you accuse my friend of this behavior!" is a sample retort, which leads to the most common retaliatory behavior: the Silent Treatment. (The most damaging example is firing an employee who makes a harassment complaint.)

The scope of this issue is a national one, and it has been around for too long in our employment history. We define sexual or racial harassment in the workplace as an unwanted behavior that is directed at a library employee, typically by a patron who violates personal and professional boundaries, by going beyond normal conversation and social interaction that becomes sexually and racially offensive. All employees have the right to a work environment that does not allow sexual or racial harassment (or retaliation) from anyone, including directors, managers, supervisors, coworkers, colleagues, vendors, visitors, or patrons. Our library employees need to tell our personnel stakeholders if these behaviors are happening to them or around them so the library director and/or HR can address them, investigate them, and stop them.

If we look at library patrons in terms of their behavior we first ask, "Does this language impact the business of our library? Must library staff tolerate this language as part of their interaction with certain patrons?" The answers to both, of course, are yes and no. These comments hurt our business, and no employee should have to hear them. Saying this and making it so can be challenging. Some patrons will even deny they said anything, but we will begin by looking at the patron's behavioral history in our library (in our Security Incident Reports) and by believing our employees.

SETTING BOUNDARIES

The first line of defense in these types of situations starts with the library employee, who should say to the patron, "Don't talk to me that way. Don't ask me these types of questions. I will not answer them. I will not answer any personal questions or tolerate any sexual or racial remarks from you. I'll do my job on your behalf in terms of helping you with what you need from the library, but I won't put up with that type of behavior."

My favorite approaches for pestering patrons are these two: "I have to go and help other patrons" or, if no one else is around, "I need to go and do another part of my job." It's hard for the patron to dispute those statements as you walk away.

Sometimes just putting that person on notice immediately once these things come to your attention solves the problem. It's for those specific situations where this person's behavior does not stop or the employee is intimidated or fearful about confronting this person that library leaders need to get involved.

And with these assertive approaches, employees can set immediate boundaries with the patron, and it may solve the problem the first time. Sometimes, however, as we have seen (and I have heard lots of stories from around the country), library patrons will continue to push the envelope by asking personal questions or making sexually or racially harassing comments that they think are okay or appropriate when, in reality, they know that they're not appropriate and this needs to stop. These patrons like to be provocative and annoying, and they want to see what they can get away with.

Let's talk a bit about what more severe boundaries look like for these perpetrators of sexual/racial harassment, including being banned from the library for some prescribed amount of time or even being kicked out permanently. We can also set behavioral boundaries while still allowing the patrons to use the library, but with supervision and control: "Sir, you'll conduct your library business only online, by telephone, or here, with designated supervisors. We're not allowing you to engage with our employees here, based on your previous comments or behaviors. You can still use the library, but you won't be interacting with our employees without our supervision."

We want supervisors to address these events as soon as they come to their attention. As I've seen, one way to start a successful solution to the problem is when several employees will come to their boss together and have a group conversation, describing what this particular patron is saying or doing around them and how they want it to stop. This proves that talking with your colleagues collectively about a patron's behavior may be useful to create consequences. This is especially true because each employee may have a different experience, making it much more difficult for the patron to deny these behaviors.

THE VALUE OF MULTIPLE CHANNELS OF REPORTING AND THE INVESTIGATIVE PROCESS

One of the most useful tools for harassment prevention is called "multiple channels of reporting." This means if you are sexually or racially harassed by anyone in the library workspace, you have the right to speak to your boss, your boss's boss, the library director, or the HR office in your library, if you have one. You can also go to an elected or appointed official in your city or county, or the city or town attorney, district attorney, or county counsel. We need to tell our leaders in responsible charge positions (inside and outside of the library), elected or appointed officials, and all people who work in supervisory positions that they're responsible for hearing sexual or racial harassment reports when they come to their attention. The reason for this is obvious. When we say to an employee the only person you can report sexual or racial harassment to is your boss and your boss is the one doing the harassment, then the employee probably won't report it. You should be able to go to any number of directors, managers, or supervisors, and if you feel more comfortable speaking to somebody who is not your direct boss, that's fine. Speak to that person. You don't have to go through the "chain of command"; you can talk to anybody inside your organization who is in a responsible supervisory position, in a leadership role, to get some help for your concerns.

Any reports of harassment in the library should trigger an investigative inquiry process. This could range from a conversation about an issue that has been handled successfully by the employee to a response that could involve HR representatives, private investigators, or attorneys, depending on the scope and seriousness. It's done to determine if there was a policy violation of your rights to fair and harassment-free treatment as an employee. Besides getting your side of the events, the library director, manager, or supervisor may speak to other supervisors or employees about what they have seen or heard and look at incident reports that have been gathered about this patron's past behaviors.

Once the data has been gathered, it may be necessary to carefully confront the patron. For example, "It's come to my attention you sexually or racially harassed our employee, one or more times, with this type of specific language or behavior. We cannot and I will not allow this to continue if you still wish to receive services from this library."

We put the patron on notice at that point, and we give him a warning not to continue the comments or behavior. For low-level, single-incident harassment situations where there has been no physical contact, a verbal warning to the patron may solve the problem. Or we may need to create a written warning and ban the person for some span of time and/or change the way we provide services to the patron.

It's possible a patron may have harassed several employees, across other branches or other parts of the library. This is why we need to have staff meetings with our supervisors and our leadership team to say we as a group have concerns about this patron's behavior, we have concerns about this patron's interactions with a lot of us, and it needs to stop. Sometimes the supervisors don't always hear the full story, they don't always see the impact of the issue, and they don't realize how serious or, in some cases, how systemic it is around the organization. They need to know about multiple events with multiple employee targets, and they need to address them.

STALKING IN THE LIBRARY SPACE

Certain patron behaviors connected to sexual or racial harassment could fall under the legal definition of stalking. As a crime, stalking is a felony in all fifty states. In 1990, California legislators, supported by advice and assistance from law enforcement and a lot of celebrity victims, wrote the first stalking law in the United States. The rest of the states followed the California statutory language as they rolled out their own versions in the following years.

For stalking to be a crime, the victim has to be in "real or sustained fear for his or her life." If you tell the police, "Yes, he bothers me but I'm not afraid of him," then they usually won't be able to make an arrest for stalking. Another element of the crime is that the perpetrator's behavior has to have happened over a span of time. One event is not always stalking, unless several instances happen right in a row, even over one day. Usually, however, police and prosecutors are looking for a "pattern of behavior over a span of time."

I frequently tell employees in the library that it's kind of ironic that we're in an information-providing business and sometimes these perpetrators use your internet, your Google searches to find out information about you personally.

I'm not a huge fan of name tags with the employee's full name on them. I like your first name and your title; sometimes we see a lot of information that you can get from a first and last name in Google. You say to yourself as a library employee, "Well, my personal information is pretty well hidden and I don't have a big social media following" or "I'm not on social media that much," and then you find out that you signed up on some checklist, somewhere in some store or you put your name and address on the list at church and that gets scanned up on the internet and that's how this person figures out where you live. I have seen situations of sexual or racial harassment escalate to the point where the patron is confronting or following or stopping the employee in the parking lot before he or she comes to work or after they leave for work. I've seen situations evolve into stalking as well.

Stalking is a set of behaviors done by the perpetrator designed to make the person on the receiving end feel afraid for their safety. Stalking is not just an irritating thing; it's a fear-creating thing. It's not just something where you say, "I wish this person would go away and leave me alone." What you're saying is, "I'm fearful this person is going to harm me." And that's a big difference from other types of sexual or racial harassment we have seen.

I say this to library employees all the time: "If you have any interactions with patrons outside of work that make you feel fearful—like they somehow discover where you live and come by your house, or have stopped you at the gym, or have seen you at the grocery store—you must, must, must tell your supervisor immediately, including the library director, and it's a situation that's going to involve the police."

The police's function in these situations is to investigate these things, figure out whether this person has a criminal background or the kind of background where you may be in jeopardy of being harmed, and inform us about what we need to do in terms of intervention to get this person to stop bothering you (to the point where you're fearful of going to work, or leaving your car in the parking lot, or coming in or going out of your facility). That's when stalking is a serious issue.

Many times people ask me about the violence potential with stalking, and for the most part, what I have seen in my career is that stalking is most likely to turn to violence any time there was previous sexual intimacy between the target and the suspect (the "I can't have you, nobody else can" kind of guy). If there was no previous sexual intimacy between the target and the suspect, violence is much less likely and, in fact, quite rare in those types of stalking situations. Most of those perpetrators are typically irritating, creepy, immature people who can't control their space and boundaries around other folks, and they develop sort of a target list where they come after people who infatuate them.

When it comes to revealing personal information I think you have to be firm and assertive and even sometimes not very polite when telling somebody "I'm not going to tell you whether I'm married. I'm not going to tell you whether I'm dating. I'm not going to tell you anything about my personal life. I'm not going to tell you whether I have any kids or what neighborhood I live in; I'm just not going to do it. I'll be happy to do my job on your behalf and to help you with information or services that you need when you come to the library, but I'm not giving you personal information about my life."

Don't be afraid to be direct. Don't be subtle; be assertive. Like bullies, harassers and stalkers have an intuitive way of reading weakness in their targets. Although our parents may have told us to be nice to strangers (e.g., Santa, the Easter Bunny, Chuck E. Cheese, Minnie, Mickey, and Goofy, etc.), sometimes you have to be assertively rude to safeguard your personal information when somebody keeps chipping away at it in an attempt to find out things about you that they should not know.

WORST-CASE PATRON BEHAVIORAL SCENARIOS: RESTRAINING ORDERS

Let's talk about the more serious consequence for a patron for harassing language, physical contact, or stalking behaviors, which would be the use of a civil restraining order, often known as a stay-away order or a Temporary Restraining Order (TRO). Some of these court orders will ban the patron for up to one year; some for up to three years.

For that to happen, we've got to have a collection of their behaviors over a span of time, which will point to a pattern where a civil court judge will agree that the order needs to be approved, served to the person, and enforced by the police and, if necessary, the court, using a contempt of court violation as the charge.

Typically the restraining order process happens when the patron is served with a subpoena that requests him or her to appear in court to answer the complaint from the library. The city, county, district, or town attorney will make their claim as to why we need a restraining order to protect our library staff, our facilities, and other patrons from this person's continued behavior. The accused person can make his or her argument to the judge as to why he or she shouldn't be restrained, and the judge will decide. Sometimes these people don't show up at the restraining order hearing, in which case the judge will issue the order by default judgment.

SEXUAL AND RACIAL HARASSMENT RECAP

Don't wait for harassment issues to solve themselves. They rarely go away without some form of intervention, first, by the employee telling the patron to stop the conduct and, second, by his or her supervisor or director stepping in to reinforce that harassment is against library policy and will not be tolerated.

Have the courage to report. We can't fix what we don't know about. Share your concerns with coworkers as well. We have a responsibility to protect each other from harassing patrons. What has happened to you may be happening to another employee.

Create consequences for the perpetrator. Set new behavioral boundaries. "You will only interact with a supervisor or me for your library needs. You will not make any contact with any employee, inside or outside the branch, in any way. If you do, our next step will be to ban you from the branch or get a civil restraining order against you." Or the patron can only do business with the library over the phone or over the internet.

Managers and supervisors need to provide support for targeted employees, including time off, access to Employee Assistance Program (EAP) counseling services, and relocation inside the facility or to a new branch if they request it (and not as a retaliatory move).

For employees, have patience through the investigative process. The more complex the situation is and the longer it has gone on, the more lengthy the investigation may be.

Directors and supervisors will need to monitor patron interactions as best as they can, and remind all staff that they have the right to work in a harassment-free workplace.

4

Better Responses for Patrons Dealing with Homelessness

AN EMPATHY-DRIVEN UNDERSTANDING

Much of my wise counsel on this tough topic comes from my American Library Association (ALA) colleague and homeless expert/author Ryan Dowd, Esq. His 2018 ALA book, *The Librarian's Guide to Homelessness: An Empathy-Driven Approach to Solving Problems, Preventing Conflict, and Serving Everyone*, is my bible when it comes to providing advice to library staff. Besides being an attorney, for many decades Ryan was the executive director of Hesed House, one of the biggest homeless shelters in the state of Illinois. He started working there as a volunteer at thirteen and is their leader in spirit and actions. He agrees with me that the difference between the phrases "homeless patron" versus "patron experiencing homelessness" is not what we need to focus on: it's all about treating them with dignity and empathy, getting them the help they ask for, and keeping them and all other patrons safe.

He and I also agree that progress with the chronically homeless population can be slow. Besides being a traumatized population, they are also a "treatment-resistant" population, a term social workers, crisis counselors, and mental health clinicians use to talk about a group of people that will not always reach out for the lifelines we offer them. As just one example, when we place some chronically homeless individuals (who have spent decades living on the streets) into a hotel for the night, they sleep on the floor instead of the bed.

As such, in this chapter and others, I will refer to patrons experiencing homelessness as either homeless patrons or homeless individuals. The first suggests they are in your library, the second that they are in our communities. It is not directed as a slur, a label, or a value judgment of something that could be impacting their lives for a short duration (only a few weeks) or as a chronic condition (decades). If you feel strongly about my misuse of these words, substitute the phrase you prefer, and let's keep going.

No issue—and I mean no issue—related to library security brings up as many strong feelings as does dealing with homeless patrons. As you might expect if you work in a library or consider library employees' differing points of view, these feelings fall along a spectrum from "We need to help all homeless patrons; they are human beings too" to "Some of them really scare me and I wish they wouldn't come into my library every day." I don't disagree with either perspective and I'd ask you to suspend your judgment about one end of this range or the other simply because what has happened to you has not happened to them and vice versa. If your experiences with homeless patrons are mostly positive, with only a few outliers who have exhibited bad, threatening, or violent behavior, then you have one set of feelings about their presence in your library. If you have been threatened or assaulted by one or more potentially or actually dangerous homeless patrons, then your view is more toward the other side of the spectrum.

By no means do I say all homeless patrons are dangerous or even have the potential to be dangerous. In my experience, most homeless individuals in and around the libraries are docile, largely cooperative when treated fairly, and want to avoid confrontations that will get them kicked out of the library, banned, arrested, or have their personal stuff impounded or destroyed.

But because I am like a dermatologist, who rarely sees healthy skin, many of my collected stories about homeless patrons come from library employees, supervisors, managers, and directors who have had really negative experiences with them.

This doesn't mean that this chapter will focus on the negative, only that every experience with a homeless person on the street or a homeless patron in the library falls inside a certain context. And speaking of context, since I'm a big fan of Dr. Drew Pinsky (www.drdrew.com) and listen to his podcasts almost daily, I take a lot of my statistical data from him, largely because he has worked with that population in Los Angeles for many decades. In my long career, I have seen enough examples of good and bad homeless behavior myself, some success stories initiated by hardworking and compassionate people, some spectacular failures, and a lot of national and local hand-wringing and saying, "What do we need to do that will really have an impact for this troubled population?"

THE THREE TYPES OF HOMELESS INDIVIDUALS, PER RYAN DOWD

I take my information on the overall homeless population from Ryan Dowd, and in our conversations he has defined the types of people who find themselves in some form of homelessness (living in their cars, in a shelter, in a subsidized hotel, on the street) in three ways:

About 50 percent of people on the street are homeless for less than two weeks. They don't have a major life issue that interferes with their ability to get off the street. They can get access to social and financial support from friends or family around them. Their brief stint being homeless often came after a series of consecutive catastrophes: promised a new job, moved to a new city with their family, everything they own gets stolen from their car, and the job disappears. It is their relationships and their desire to get off the street as quickly as possible that help them do so.

About 40 percent of people on the street are homeless for two weeks up to one year. They have one major life issue, typically substance abuse/addiction or untreated mental health problems. Both life issues together (see below) are intensely challenging and can keep them trapped in homelessness until they can get or ask for help.

And about 10 percent of people on the streets are homeless for more than one year and up to twenty or more years. They have two major life issues, typically substance abuse/addiction and mental health problems. As Ryan has said from his own observations, many of this third category have bipolar disorders, schizophrenia, depression, anger issues, and/or overwhelming anxiety; they even can be on the autism spectrum and may or may not have ever been diagnosed for that particular issue.

Their mental health concerns, when mixed with opiates, fentanyl, methamphetamine, and alcohol can make them unpredictable. This is even more so when they are in withdrawal from these drugs.

Withdrawal from opiates and fentanyl (which starts about four to six hours after a longtime user's last dose) is like having the worst case of the flu times ten—nausea, diarrhea, vomiting, body aches, extreme anxiety, that feeling like their skin is crawling. It's quite unpleasant, and they may even act out aggressively because they aren't thinking clearly and are worried the police will arrest them. Having to quit drugs cold turkey in jail is not a fun ten days.

Withdrawal from methamphetamine is even more crazy making. The person feels agitated, anxious, fearful, and quite paranoid. This can lead to irrational behaviors and irrational statements of the conspiracy theory type.

Withdrawal from longtime alcohol use can have serious health consequences, including seizures, convulsions, and even sudden death. People in treatment for alcoholism will need careful medical supervision and specific medications to cope. Many homeless people who want to stop drinking only do so when their livers start to fail.

You're probably not too surprised to learn that the police most often encounter this third group, in the library, other public locations, retail stores, or on the streets. Their fears and anxieties when encountering the police don't always end well for both parties.

So what do we do, as librarians, with this information about the 50, 40, and 10 percent homeless populations? Asking careful, polite, compassionate, empathic questions, or responding to the comments or admissions made by someone who might be homeless can fill in your knowledge.

If the patron seems clear eyed and clear headed and is asking you about how to get access to support services because they just came into town and are facing difficulties, you might have someone in the 50 percent category. Your immediate support here—offering resources and tips and tricks that you have gathered over your career—can get this person (and their accompanying family) back on their feet quickly. A few examples include, "Have you tried this place? Do you know anything about this agency? Do you have any friends or family in town we can call for you?"

If the patron seems to be facing some drug/alcohol or mental health challenges (but not both, which can be difficult to distinguish), and they admit to being on the streets a short time and under a year, then you know they may be in the second category and will need more specific referrals to sobriety or mental health programs.

For the patrons in the third category, progress can be slow, and their successes often reverse themselves (they get arrested for fighting, they leave treatment, they stop taking their medications because they hate the side effects, they quit going to group therapy or their Alcoholics Anonymous / Narcotics Anonymous meetings). If they know you, like you, and trust you, you may be able to get them to start on the path to health and recovery again.

THE POTENTIALLY DANGEROUS HOMELESS PATRON TRIANGLE: A DIFFERENT TYPE OF PERSON EXPERIENCING HOMELESSNESS

There is a disconnect between the way some employees perceive patrons experiencing homelessness and homeless patrons who display what I define as the "Dangerous Behavior Triad." The first, much larger group, is mostly docile, wants to follow the rules, doesn't want to be hassled by library security or the police, and doesn't want to be kicked out of the library by staff.

The second, much smaller group, displays three problematic behaviors:

1. They are actively mentally ill (psychotic, paranoid, out of touch with reality, angrily suspicious).
2. They are actively under the influence of street or prescription drugs (especially stimulant drugs) and/or alcohol, to the degree that their lack of sobriety makes them erratic and violent.
3. They are actively predatory in their behavior—they ask for money in aggressive ways, they threaten others with their size or strength, and they aren't deterred by a staff member or library security, or even the police.

They will not cooperate when asked to leave. They often fight the cops who are trying to get them to leave and they are aggressively prone to act up and act out. All too often they are sexual predators as well, falling into a disturbing category known as being a "try-sexual," meaning they will try to force themselves sexually on anyone—adult males, adult females, or children. Most homeless people who have lived on the streets for a long span of time are fearful of these people because they are often targeted by them too.

I see more and more of these predatory types at libraries today, and staff needs to know how to deal with them while they wait for the arrival of the police. They are used to bullying or scaring people to get what they want (food, money, goods, sex). You need to be cautious, be more assertive than usual, and use good judgment about keeping space and distance between you and them. Their behavior may require you to isolate them in some part of the room—get other patrons and staff out and away—until the police arrive. It's not uncommon for them to break things and smash furniture when their anger takes over, and they sometimes do decide to leave before the cops get there. Your interactions with them are probably going to need to be more cautious than with other homeless patrons.

HOMELESSNESS AS A FAILURE OF RELATIONSHIPS

I am and always will be a lifelong introvert. (I've seen some of you at our weekly Introverts Anonymous meetings: "Hi, I'm Steve and I'm an introvert." Hi, Steve!")

But even if I'm an introvert trapped in an extrovert's profession—public speaking—I have the good sense to surround myself with quality, nontoxic, supportive, loving friends and family, who would help me if I were in real dire straits financially, or suddenly living outdoors.

I have several dear friends who I have known for thirty, forty, or even fifty years, who would drop what they are doing and fly to New York City and wait for me at the top of the Empire State Building, no questions asked, if I simply requested they be there. Perhaps you have similar people in your life, and it's a blessing if you do.

For the homeless population in Ryan Dowd's third category—especially the 10 percenters—they do not have the safety net of these supportive relationships. Through bad luck, the devastating impact of the two major life issues working against them at once, and the destruction of relationships (their fault) or abandonment by friends and family (the fault of others), they have no support and so their spiral begins.

Sometimes they can get treatment, and sometimes they will finally surrender to treatment themselves; but long-term, chronic homelessness can be a fatal disease. Opiate use, alcoholism, and constant battles with other street people (especially the predatory types mentioned earlier) lead them to die on the street (three to six deaths per day is a number Dr. Drew Pinsky uses for Los Angeles County[1]).

Consider how the homeless person, especially in the second and third Ryan Dowd categories, have broken their relationships with this long list of potential supporters who could help get them off the streets. It's not uncommon for people in this person's life, who have been patient, to suddenly say, "I will do no more. He or she will have to sink or swim alone." For the chronically

Better Responses for Patrons Dealing with Homelessness

homeless, with decades on the streets, these relationships can seem like a distant memory, fading every day.

INNER AND EXTENDED FAMILY

Parents, siblings, grandparents, their birth and stepchildren, aunts and uncles, nieces and nephews, cousins, and others have all stepped away, often heartbroken but resolute not to keep shoveling the sand against the tide.

SPOUSE OR INTIMATE PARTNER

There is no further contact from a husband or wife or boyfriend or girlfriend.

RECENT BOSSES, FORMER EMPLOYERS, EX-COWORKERS

Often these people have had the homeless person break promises about getting treatment, or they have stolen from the organization.

LANDLORDS

They have evicted the person and will not welcome them back.

FRIENDS

They have lost patience and given up hope.

SOCIAL SERVICES PROVIDERS, SOCIAL WORKERS, AND MENTAL HEALTH AND SUBSTANCE ABUSE PROFESSIONALS AND CLINICIANS

These hardworking and dedicated professionals have stunning numbers of cases. It's not unusual for one social worker in a large city to have more than one hundred cases. They can only triage and work with the ones they can help the most.

HOUSING AUTHORITIES

Like the landlords, they have grown weary of the homeless person violating the rules at the residences where they have been put. Like the social workers, they move on to the person with the next greatest need who will not trash the room, sell drugs, or fight with other tenants.

LIBRARIES

This book has told this story many times about how you can only do what you can only do. It's important to not stop caring or care too much. The balance in between is what keeps you motivated and sane.

HOMELESS SHELTERS

There are a lot of rules in some homeless shelters and not many in others. Sometimes some homeless people will not or just can't follow them. As one example, some homeless shelters will not accept a person who is actively on drugs or drunk; others will. Some require the shelter residents to participate in sober living activities, listen to religious lectures, or seek some form of treatment; others don't.

FAITH-BASED AND COMMUNITY SUPPORT GROUPS

Think of all the public, private, and grant-funded agencies that exist to provide help: the Salvation Army; St. Vincent de Paul; Catholic, Methodist, and Lutheran charities; national coalitions for homelessness; and state programs. These agencies have rules, too.

THE CRIMINAL JUSTICE SYSTEM

Cops, courts, prosecutors, probation officers, parole officers, judges, and victims' advocate groups have all given up and moved on to the next case, the next perpetrators, the next victims.

FEDERAL AID, STATE OR LOCAL PROGRAMS, OR GOVERNMENT PROVIDERS (DMV, EDD, SSI, SSDI)

Think about how hard it would be to function in our world without a driver's license, a state-issued ID card, or a birth certificate needed to get either. Many homeless people fall through the cracks and don't have the knowledge or patience to wait in long lines for federal and state aid. The system moves on without them.

AND THE LIBRARY 2.0 SURVEY SAYS . . .

As part of a webinar recording project in 2019, Steve Hargadon, my training partner and the founder of Library 2.0, conducted a brief survey of 130 library employees about to listen to my webinar on homeless individuals at the library. He asked for their comments on an open-ended question about their interactions with the homeless as part of their work. The purpose of his question was to gather as much comment/anecdotal data as possible, so we could review it before my webinar workshop. A collection of their responses are listed verbatim here.

I wasn't really surprised to see the comments split fairly evenly along two distinct conclusions: (1) "We should see people experiencing homelessness as human beings, serve their needs, and have empathy." (2) "Some homeless people cause quite a lot of problems and can be disruptive and scary."

The following are some examples from the first, more humanitarian category:

"Homeless people deserve dignity and they are often treated as dirt. I don't care why they are homeless and I don't care if it's a choice or not. I don't care if they're addicts. They are people. They deserve to use public spaces. Being homeless doesn't mean you're a criminal or scary. I want to see better practices that help homeless people have agency and make their own decisions."

"It's not appropriate (or it's discriminatory) to distinguish someone's housing—mansion, apartment, or homeless. It's whether or not they are adhering to library policy."

"Language matters and influences perceptions: One thing that's important to remember is homelessness is not an identity, it's a condition."

Here are some examples from the second, more pragmatic category:

"How do you set appropriate boundaries for staff (who are usually not trained social workers), yet also maintain a welcoming, helpful space for homeless patrons? How to honor the concerns of other patrons while still remaining open for all?"

"The public library is for everyone. We all know this. But sometimes it seems like we're so busy being tolerant of the homeless population's myriad problems that we are alienating people in our community who are capable of using the library without harassing, offending, or disturbing others around them."

We can have a lot of discussion between these two endpoints on the spectrum.

Here are the primary concerns many library staffers had about the homeless population in their facilities. (I'm well aware that people who "look homeless" are not and people who "don't look homeless" can be. We shouldn't judge a book by its cover, but sometimes the truth—about a person's perceived living conditions—is the truth.) For lack of a better phrase, this next section could be called: "Behavioral Issues Caused by Some Homeless Patrons."

Health, sanitation, bed bugs, diseases, body odors, and hygiene.
Drug and alcohol use, possession of paraphernalia, and drug sales.
Sleeping in the library.
Hiding out in the building overnight.
Mental health, emotional health issues, crying.
Disruptive drug- or alcohol-induced threats, assaults, or violence.
Threats (especially against student workers).
Fighting amongst themselves.
Possession of weapons.
Safety of the homeless with domestic violence issues.
Safety of staff, patrons, neighboring schools, parking lots, at nighttime.
Blocking aisles and emergency exits with their bags and belongings, especially in small libraries or small rooms.
Unwanted sexual advances.
Security and/or police response times are too slow; problem patrons take advantage of these delays.
Thefts of library, staff, or patron property.
Not understanding, not following, or not caring about the library's guidelines for behavior.
Use of restrooms for personal showers and washing clothing.

Use of the library as a regular eating place.
Can need extensive support with computer applications, filling out forms, and such.
How to help provide them with opportunities to move forward: life issues, finances, food, security?
Lack of trained staff and resources after cutbacks and reduced staffing.
Students who are homeless.

What follows next we can define as rhetorical questions/common comments from the Library 2.0 survey responders about interacting with homeless patrons. Some of these are requests for help:

"We don't have resources, training, consistent policies, or procedures."

"What to actually do when the homeless are sleeping on our back steps?"

"If our county doesn't have services or they are far away, the library becomes the main place. The public's perception of the library with homeless men hanging out on a regular basis. The library can be seen as a day shelter by the public. People are afraid to enter the library when it is filled with lots of the homeless."

"Our county sees libraries as a solution for homelessness instead of providing other shelters or services themselves. The cuts in social services impacting the library require more staff interventions, which can cause burnout."

"Does providing services encourage more of the same? (When we provide services, are we inviting people not to take responsibility for their own circumstances?)"

"Not enough help or support from county social and mental health services. (How about having a social services resource desk in the library?) In some cases, there are simply no resources at all in the area."

"We need options to give people who are in need of shelter. What nongovernmental resources are available? Churches and other organizations?"

"We don't have a way to give library cards to those without a permanent address."

"My board prefers to believe that we don't have those issues."

"Those needing assistance are not getting it. Not getting shelter, food, showers, mental health, addiction recovery services."

"Community perceptions and approaches to homelessness are lacking."

"How do we work at a community level to address root causes?"

"How to enforce policies, especially when it makes staff feel vulnerable?"

"How to address specific and often highly personal requests for help by the homeless (e.g., being asked for a ride after closing time)?"

"How to treat those who are homeless with kindness and respect, including when setting healthy boundaries. How to make sure they feel welcome and are included. How to make sure they aren't treated differently because of stigma. How to avoid bias or discrimination."

Better Responses for Patrons Dealing with Homelessness

"Understanding the variety of reasons someone can be homeless. Being careful in how it is discussed."

"How to help staff and patrons see those who are homeless as equally deserving of access."

"How to help other patrons feel welcome and safe while still providing services to the homeless."

"How to respond to children living in cars/tents/etc. who have panhandling parents: helping versus reporting?"

"Providing more and better spaces and facilities for homeless patrons."

"We want metal detectors on public floors."

"We wear security buttons that can be pushed."

"We have a prepared sheet with services and contacts we give them."

"How to communicate and interact so situations de-escalate instead of escalate."

"How to respond to patrons who are concerned or upset about homeless in libraries or homelessness in general. These are tricky conversations."

"Should our library create staff positions or specific resources?"

"Providing more and better spaces and facilities for homeless patrons."

"It helps us to have a system that cuts off the computers at closing."

SO WHAT CAN YOU DO AS A LIBRARY PROFESSIONAL?

There is no one instant answer and certainly no easy answers to the homeless crisis in our country. From a library perspective, I see our responses at both the macro (big-picture) and micro (one-on-one) levels. From a macro perspective, I have always felt libraries can provide the most help by organizing the various community stakeholders for the homeless, to come together on at least a quarterly basis for meetings at the library to share best practices, offer ideas to the library staff and each other, and make a commitment to keep on coming back together.

The list of the various entities in the community who have a stake in helping the homeless is a long one, including social workers and county social services, homeless shelters, mental health advocates, substance abuse treatment professionals, law enforcement, housing specialists, vocational specialists, and private-sector or grant-funded charities, to name a few. Getting these people to the library meeting table on a scheduled basis is not easy; people change jobs, move on, and lose interest in the discussion, and then the progress from the previous conversations can fade. In my Perfect Library World, the library leaders and interested staff members would generate the necessary enthusiasm to bring these experts together at least several times per year with the goal to make forward progress.

From an interaction standpoint, the rules of engagement with patrons who admit to homelessness or show the signs of having to live their lives on the streets are the same as with other potentially challenging patrons:

Using the Essential Eight: firm, fair, consistent, assertive, legal, empathic, patient, and reasonable treatment, like all people should expect from us. Recall my Ten Core Questions to ask and answer.

Setting boundaries, in line with our Code of Conduct and behavioral policies.

Paying attention to your use of space and distance, not touching or blocking them, not touching their personal belongings (or throwing them away), creating an exit path for them or you to leave if the conversation turns confrontational. Protecting yourself by using proxemic barriers or disengaging and leaving, as necessary.

Using alignment to find the best fit between the patron and the staff member. If it's you, then use your communication and service tools and do your job. If a colleague or a supervisor or manager is a better conversational fit, then let them handle it.

Using a lighter touch, even a bit of a sense of humor, to help the person see you as just someone who is trying to get through the day as well.

Asking for compliance and reminding yourself and the homeless patron that tomorrow is another day and a chance for better rule following. You will probably see this person again and again, so it's useful to keep the long game in mind.

TWO CLOSING MESSAGES OF THIS CHAPTER FROM MY FRIEND, RYAN DOWD

In these pages, I have written about Ryan Dowd's lifelong efforts to help the homeless. Below, I have collected powerful and parting thoughts from him, designed to give us hope for this complex and often tragic community issue:

CAN WE SOLVE THE HOMELESS PROBLEM IN AMERICA?

Here are his thoughts:

> Don't believe the cynics. We can end homelessness in our country. Homelessness is not inevitable. It did not always exist. The current phenomenon of homelessness, as we understand it today, did not exist until about 40 years ago. Very few shelters existed before 1980; now they're everywhere. Homelessness is a very modern invention, and is the confluence of bad policies and shifting societal attitudes about family responsibility. If we can create homelessness in a matter of decades, is it really absurd to think that we can't end it in the same amount of time?[2]

In our correspondence, he offers these contemplations:

> I have seen countless individuals lose all hope. They accept that they will be homeless for their entire lives.
> There is a predictable pattern:

First, they lose faith in others. They accept that the world is a hostile place and that they are the only one that can look out for their own interests.

Next, they lose faith in themselves. They accept that they have no ability to change a cold, harsh world.

Finally, cynicism becomes a form of "wisdom." In the face of insurmountable odds, hope seems irrational and naïve.

I have also seen countless individuals discover hope again. They find the courage to see a different future for themselves and their families. Here, too, there is a pattern:

It starts in the dark. It begins deep in the human soul for no apparent reason other than the miracle that is the human spirit. Against all odds, a coal from a long-dead fire begins to glow and give off heat.

At first, it looks foolish. When an alcoholic with slurred speech declares that he will get sober, it can sound absurd. When hope is in its infancy, people mock it.

As it grows, hope comes under attack by cynics with an agenda. Friends, family, or strangers try to undermine recovery for their own selfish ends. Misery loves company.

Finally, hope wins. In retrospect, what had looked inconceivable appears inevitable.

My friends, I don't offer my observations on hope as mere intellectual curiosity. Our country has lost hope.

We have lost faith in others. We have accepted that our country is a hostile divided place, and we must each look out for our own interests.

We have lost faith in ourselves. We have resigned ourselves to the fact that we are unable to effect change.

We have mistaken cynicism for wisdom. Internet pundits compete to sell the bleakest vision of our future.

Fortunately, we have experts in our midst. Perhaps we can all learn how to hope from our homeless neighbors. Just maybe, the most vulnerable can show the way forward.

Our country's healing will begin in darkness. When our collective spirit can no longer tolerate division and fear, we will begin to change.

At first, it will look foolish. Even writing this, it feels silly to even think about a country without a deep partisan divide.

Before hope wins, cynics will attack it. We must learn to ignore pundits and politicians who profit from our fear of one another.

Hope will win; it seems inconceivable now, but it always does . . .

My friends, we find greatness together, or not at all. Peace, Ryan Dowd.[3]

NOTES

1. https://drdrew.com/2022/los-angeles-homeless-can-street-medicine-prevent-a-healthcare-crisis-w-dr-michael-hochman-ask-dr-drew/. July 28, 2022.
2. Ryan Dowd, *The Librarian's Guide to Homelessness: An Empathy-Driven Approach to Solving Problems, Preventing Conflict, and Serving Everyone* (Chicago: ALA Editions, 2018), p. 238.
3. Author's personal correspondence. May 3, 2021.

5

Dealing with Patrons with Mental Health and Substance Use Disorders

BEHAVIORAL AND MEDICAL EVENTS

A TRAUMA-INFORMED LIBRARY COMMUNITY

This chapter looks at mental health concerns and drug/alcohol use with certain patrons and how—like interacting with some homeless patrons—it can be challenging to provide service and focus on the safety of all. Not every drunk patron is problematic. Not every street drug-using patron is dangerous. And we know from more than a century of research that not every person struggling with mental health issues is violent. But in my work, some of these three behaviors come together, and it can create safety and security problems. It's hard to communicate, reason with, or negotiate with people who are not thinking clearly because of drugs, alcohol, or mental health problems.

We already know we can't pick our customers. We are a public space and we get who we get. Successfully managing problematic behaviors and still serving patrons who have one, two, or all three of these issues (and add in a trauma background, so common, and discussed) requires certain tools for your tool kit.

So much of what we see in this country that is connected to mental health and substance use has its origins in the trauma the person was exposed to, most often as a child. The combination of alcohol, legal and illegal drug use, and mental health problems interweaves itself through every part of the person's life, with the first two often used to mask the pain of the last. Both concerns make it hard to function and live a long and happy life, and most definitely so without medical or behavioral treatment, support from others, and no small amount of personal courage. Drug and alcohol addiction can be a fatal condition.

Mental illness, to the degree where depression and suicidal ideations become overwhelming, leads some people to make fatal decisions, which scar their families for generations. (To put it into literary context, Ernest Hemingway, who struggled with alcoholism, multiple brain injuries, and depression, killed himself, as did his father, his sister, his brother, one of his sons, and his granddaughter. Talk about a tragic family legacy.)

The US government office leading our national understanding of both drug abuse and mental illness is called SAMHSA, or the Substance Abuse and Mental Health Services Administration (www.SAMHSA.gov). Its leaders and researchers continue to study the impact of trauma on the lives of people who suffer from one or both issues, and this has led to a concept called "trauma-informed care." This suggests that the three life issues—trauma, substance use disorders, and mental health—are related, and it makes sense when we consider how people with untreated trauma and mental health issues use drugs and alcohol to cope, with unsuccessful results.

A July 2014 report from SAMHSA, titled "Concept of Trauma and Guidance for a Trauma-Informed Approach," explains how it can help people in helping professions (including librarians) to understand the value of trauma-informed approaches to our interactions. It states:

> Individual trauma results from an event, series of events, or set of circumstances that is experienced by an individual as physically or emotionally harmful or life-threatening and that has lasting adverse effects on the individual's functioning and mental, physical, social, emotional, or spiritual well-being. A program, organization, or system that is trauma-informed realizes the widespread impact of trauma and understands potential paths for recovery; recognizes the signs and symptoms of trauma in clients, families, staff, and others involved with the system; and responds by fully integrating knowledge about trauma into policies, procedures, and practices, and seeks to actively resist re-traumatization.[1]

This issue has been covered by the American Library Association (ALA) and online and in print by various library associations, library-connected social workers, and mental health clinicians and advocates. Follow this emerging research when you consider your own response to patrons who may have mental health issues, substance abuse disorders, and/or homelessness in your library.

WHY DO PATRONS WITH MENTAL HEALTH ISSUES GO TO THE LIBRARY?

What seems obvious about this question may actually go deeper than you might first think. It goes beyond just getting out of the hot sun or the cold air. We can define people with significant mental health issues as those who have a difficult time functioning, have a hard time with social interaction, and struggle mightily with depression, anxiety, fear, hallucinations, psychoses, and the related physical health issues that can accompany these, including body pain, headaches, injuries, dehydration/hunger, blood sugar problems, and physical disabilities. We are not talking about the one in six American adults who have reported they take a psychiatrically related medication (for sleep, anxiety, depression, or hyperactivity) and can function without drawing attention to themselves.[2]

We are talking about a population that comes to your library who is unmedicated, wrongly medicated, or overmedicated, or who self-medicates with drugs and alcohol because they can't get their medications anymore or don't like the side effects. Their overt behaviors are often the issue. They come to the library to

- find a quiet, safe, peaceful space, where they can hide from their enemies, real or imagined;
- control the amount of human contact they can tolerate;
- see friends or avoid other street people;
- find a safe place to self-manage their fear, anxiety, depression, or aggression, by sitting, sleeping, or distracting themselves;
- get attention, get support, and ask for food or money;
- get intellectual stimulation, information, personal entertainment, humor, and education from the library materials and/or the internet;
- watch people;
- get relief from the danger and noise on the streets;
- avoid the police or security guards from other public places, parks, and retail shops;
- kill time because they were asked to leave for the day by family members, roommates, and shelters; or
- kill time because they are retired or are on SSDI (Social Security Disability Insurance) or SSI (Supplemental Security Income) and cannot work, even part time.

Unlike the list that follows below with patrons struggling with substance abuse, not all of this collection of behaviors is necessarily problematic, and you may not even recognize some of them as happening. If that changes, be ready to respond with service, support, boundaries, requests for better compliance, and help from your boss or colleagues if things start to escalate.

WHY DO PATRONS WITH SUBSTANCE ABUSE ISSUES GO TO THE LIBRARY?

It's a reasonable question, right? Are some of the same reasons chronic drunks and drug addicts go to the library as do mentally ill people? Yes and no. This second list is surprisingly long and makes as much sense as the first one above. Consider that substance abusers go to the library to sober up by spending time sitting or reading;

sleep it off in a library chair or couch;

use the restroom to shoot heroin or fentanyl in private;

use the restroom to manage their withdrawal symptoms (diarrhea, nausea, vomiting);

distract their forthcoming withdrawal symptoms with library materials or internet time;

buy drugs from a dealer;

sell drugs to other users;

panhandle money, cigarettes, or food from other patrons;

steal items from the library or patrons that can be pawned (liquor is cheap, street drugs can be expensive); or

stay away from the police.

It's clear from this list (and you may have come up with other examples from your own experience) that some of these behaviors are normal, don't hurt the business of the library, or don't bother you or other patrons to the point where you need to intervene. Others are illegal and dangerous. Can you tell the difference right away? Perhaps not.

As with many things we discuss in this book, it's all about the patron's behavior and how it fits into the context of the situation. Pay attention to the safety and security issues first. Assess any medical concerns. If you see the first signs of an overdose, make that fast call to paramedics.

They can always be called off if the patron rouses himself or herself and leaves. Paramedics will need to get there and do their Narcan thing if not.

If you have library security officers, they can help with some of the Code of Conduct issues or policy violations, as can you, with the support of your boss or coworkers. Some of these issues may require a police response.

A HARD DAY IN THE LIFE OF A MENTALLY ILL PERSON AT THE LIBRARY

I will say this with peace and love in my heart: some people with mental illness are troubled, and some people are troubling. Troubled people are bothered by something. People who are troubling bother people. You may encounter patrons who are one or both at your library.

Let's use the example of a mentally ill homeless man in your library who is drunk and gets belligerent with staff and other patrons when he's asked to leave. He is a big, angry guy, who has been a behavior problem several times in the past. The staff knows him by name, and while he is mostly cooperative on days when he is inside the library, today he is not. When he pushes a staff member and throws another patron's backpack on the floor, a library supervisor sends a staffer to call 9-1-1.

The man's mental illness is common among homeless individuals. He has been diagnosed as a paranoid schizophrenic, and since he is off his prescribed medications (there are many reasons why this is so: ran out, can't get more, can't afford them, refuses follow-up treatments), he uses alcohol to ease his pain and calm himself. This has predictably bad effects, resulting in erratic, confrontative, and cyclical behaviors. He is out of touch with reality and believes the world is trying to harm him. Because of his degree of paranoia, he thinks the library is out to get him and will certainly call the police to take him away.

As is common with paranoid people, they often accurately predict what will happen: "I bet you're gonna call the cops on me!" (and we do), or "I know they are gonna take me to some crazy hospital and hold me down and stab me with needles!" (which often happens as well when they are brought to an Emergency Room and given a psychiatric evaluation and a subsequent injection of a useful and necessary psychotropic medication to calm them and reorient their brains).

The police arrive and try as they might to de-escalate him or get him to go outside, but he refuses their instructions. He screams for a bit and then he sits on the floor and refuses to leave. The officers decide to try and escort him outside or, if that won't work, then handcuff him so he won't hurt them, others, or himself.

The moment the officers touch the man he starts resisting. He's not fighting with them; he's just refusing to comply, won't get up, won't put his hands behind his back. They begin to struggle with him and give him commands to stop resisting, stop fighting, and go along with being arrested. The more he struggles, the more the whole situation turns into a wrestling match. He's a big guy, and the cops are making little progress.

Any wonder why the police hate responding to these types of calls? This doesn't mean the police won't come, just that they don't like it because a lot can go wrong, and even if they do their jobs safely, the perception of bystanders is they were abusing the person.

There are a lot of issues going on with the officers in this situation. They are concerned about

- saving face (this is especially true of younger officers) and not being perceived as weak, or not in control of the situation by the subject and the public watching (who are taking videos and photographs with their smartphones);
- protecting their egos;
- exerting their legal and implied authority;
- preventing him from getting the upper hand, physically or psychologically;
- being disarmed or accidentally injuring or killing the officers or anyone else standing nearby;
- getting him safely handcuffed and outside; and
- deciding if he needs to go to a mental health hospital or the Emergency Room for a psychiatric evaluation.

At this point, let's evaluate what we know so far:

Has the mentally ill patron done enough to get himself arrested? Well, he did assault a staff member, so yes.

Can the police just disengage with him, let him sit on the floor, and even leave, and let the library staff handle it? Yes and no. Maybe he quiets and self-calms himself and finally leaves or maybe he escalates his behavior.

Will the police win this battle of compliance, one way or another? Yes. They will call for more cops to help the first two. One or more of them may use the physical tools on his or her belt, which usually include OC pepper spray (unlikely, because of the cross-contamination of other people indoors); an expandable baton (highly unlikely, as this is not a deadly force situation); Taser (possible); carotid restraint (wrongly called a "chokehold," it briefly compresses the two carotid arteries on each side of the person's neck; it's banned in most police agencies now); firearm (highly unlikely unless the subject pulls out a hidden gun or knife or succeeds in disarming either officer of his or her own gun).

What's left? Continue with verbal commands until he complies? Yes, but it's even less likely to work until all sides are exhausted from wrestling and straining against each other.

Use the "Big Blue Dogpile" (a lot of police wear blue uniforms) and swarm on top of him, fighting for control of his arms and legs until he finally gives up? Probably and most likely. These situations usually end up with the officers with torn uniforms as well as bumps, scrapes, and bruises. The subject gets the worst end of all this, leaving the room with his own bumps, scrapes, bruises, or even broken bones. Plus, it's terrifying for both sides, and it doesn't look very skilled to the observing public. (I'm not asking for your sympathy for the cops in this or any other scenario, only your empathy and a bit more understanding of their day-to-day difficulties.)

Some library staffers reading this scenario would likely reason, "Given all that is happening or could happen with this patron, should we have not called the police in the first place?" If we remove the part where the patron pushes the staff member and throws the other patron's backpack on the ground, then perhaps. But if the patron assaulted others or damaged property, our path is made more clear. There are no easy answers in those incidents where the patron's over-the-top behavior has drawn the arrival of the police. If so, we hope that the cops will do their job safely, for all concerned. If not, you have the right to make a complaint to the watch commander's office, with details of what you saw.

SAFE AND HUMANE INTERACTIONS WITH PATRONS WITH POSSIBLE MENTAL HEALTH ISSUES: KNOW THE THREE-TYPE CRITERIA

As I mentioned briefly in the introduction, the three-type criteria in all fifty states are the methods law enforcement officers, psychiatrists and psychologists, mental health clinicians, medical doctors, and social workers use to assess whether or not a person struggling with mental health issues needs to be taken to a medical or mental health facility for an evaluation. The three types include danger to self, danger to others, and gravely disabled and are not without their controversies, as clinicians, the police, mental health advocates, and family members of mentally ill people cannot always agree on who meets the criteria and what to do if they do or do not.

It's not necessary to meet all three criteria at once; only one is needed. Some people with severe mental illness may be all three at once. Others never reach the criteria and can take care of themselves, often with family, clinical, or medical support. Then there are those people who may fall through clinical assessment cracks. Here is an example:

When I lived in California and worked as a cop, the state used its Welfare and Institutions (W&I) Code 5150 to define the three types: danger to self, danger to others, or gravely disabled. The term 5150 is the usual police radio code for dispatchers to use to send officers and deputies to a home or other location where they may encounter a person suffering from debilitating mental illness. (Other police agencies, especially on the East Coast, use the term "emotionally disturbed person" [EDP] as their radio identifier for these types of calls.)

The issue arises when the officers get to a location and determine (based on their limited or even rudimentary knowledge of the three types) that the person in question is not "5150" but more like "5149 1/2." This means he or she has or is displaying problematic behaviors but doesn't meet the definition of the three types. In those situations, there is not much for the police to do but to try to get the person to calm down, leave quietly and cooperatively, or stop being a problem to those around him or her.

Fast forward to the library environment: is it possible that you deal with more patrons who are struggling with mental illness that are more likely to be 5149½ and not 5150, meaning that their behavior is not bad enough to justify calling the police, but it's still challenging for you and your colleagues and the other patrons witnessing what is happening? I will ask you to decide.

The police are not the only answer or even a useful one for those patrons whose behavior is borderline. If you can get the patron to leave or cooperate and calm himself or herself, you certainly don't need the police to come and stir up even more emotions with everyone in the library. But when those same patrons are moving into dangerous behavior or it's clear to you that they are about to be harmed, you have to make that 9-1-1 call.

WHAT ABOUT SOME OUTSIDE-THE-BOX SOCIAL SERVICES RESOURCES?

Take a moment to bless our country's social workers. It's a job that requires a specific (which means expensive) degree, a lot of on-the-job training, and exposure to many populations that desperately need help and yet fight that help every step along the way. Social workers work for counties, hospitals, elder and hospice care facilities, drug and alcohol rehabilitation facilities, and often in neighborhoods, alone, where the cops don't like to go to without backup. They deal with frightened and angry clients, as well as frightened, angry, and frustrated families, and they have a caseload that can number from the dozens to the hundreds. They are stretched too thin, often burned out, and not paid nearly enough for what they have to do.

There is a promising trend for libraries over the last few years, where social workers are being hired to work directly in the library space. This includes full-time social workers, whose only function is to meet library patrons in need and try to help them. Or they may be on a part-time basis at the library and work in other locations the rest of the week. Still others may be graduate students, who come to the library (and work for free or for a small internship stipend) as a way to build their clinical hours. If you have the luxury—and it is a luxury at this moment in time—of having any combination of these folks in your library, hang on to them with a tight grip.

We are seeing new opportunities for social workers, graduate students in psychology, public health nurses, students, interns, and similar behavioral specialists coming to work in the library, as employees, consultants, and volunteers. It's not everywhere, certainly, but it's a great start.

And what about getting help from the Veterans Administration (VA) or similar grant-funded or volunteer groups who want to work with veterans in trouble? I recall a threat assessment case I did for a city where an elderly man waved a knife at some library employees and left the building. He was quickly arrested by the police, since the station was across the municipal plaza from the library. It was clear he had cognitive issues, and his display of the knife, while it certainly could have become dangerous, was not seen by the library staff as homicidal, but more frustrated. (Again, context is everything in human behavior.) In a discussion with the safety and security stakeholders for the city as to how to handle this situation, one team member suggested we call the VA. Most of us were puzzled as to why. The team member said, "I know this guy. He's a veteran of the air force. Perhaps the VA can offer us some guidance."

So we contacted the VA, who provided a social worker for his situation. The man was fully diagnosed by a VA neurologist with dementia. He had no family and had been living alone and deteriorating rapidly. He was placed in a VA care facility. It's unlikely we would have thought to contact the VA without the safety and security team member suggesting it, because we didn't know the man's history or what services the VA could offer. That story displays a prime example of the value of group problem solving for facility security and patron behavior issues in the library space.

What about hiring psych nurses, psychotherapists, psychologists, psychiatrists, or MDs who have retired and may want to work part time in the library offering support to troubled patrons?

How about inviting directors, site managers, employees, or volunteers from a local homeless shelter to train your library staff or work on-site as volunteers for your facility?

What about offering local Alcoholics Anonymous or Narcotics Anonymous chapters to hold their meetings at the library? If you know their model, those folks will bring people who are drunk or actively on drugs to meetings if they ask to go. Perhaps they can do some outreach in your library and invite a patron with a substance abuse problem to come down to the meeting.

SUBSTANCE USE CONCERNS AND OUR LIBRARY PATRONS

According to the International Narcotics Control Board, Americans consume 99.7 percent of the world's hydrocodone supply.[3] Best known under its most common trade name, Vicodin, this drug is a powerful and addicting opiate. Some people can use it for a short time, with no lasting effects. Some people (me included) don't like it at all, because it either doesn't work on their pain, makes them edgy, gives them nightmares, or has other uncomfortable side effects, like constipation. But for other people who like this drug, they really, really like it.

The publication of Cindy Grove's ALA book, *Libraries and the Substance Abuse Crisis* (2020), reminds us of the emergence of opiate users in libraries, following the national crisis over the last ten years. She says,

> I imagine that for most of us, the idea of becoming a librarian did not include having to be on the front line of the opioid crisis. It is a fight that we did not start, but it is one that we cannot ignore or step back from. Our communities and our patrons need libraries to support them in all areas of their lives, and this crisis is no exception. We can't afford to ignore this problem. We need to seek out members of the community affected by the opioid crisis and reach out to them and support them. By reaching out, librarians have the opportunity to make profound changes in the way people struggling with addiction are treated in society and offer them a better chance of a successful recovery.[4]

We can define some terms by saying a drug is any substance, when taken into the body, that can cause physical or mental impairment. It can be legal or illegal; abused or not abused; prescribed or over the counter; natural or synthetic. Taken in excessive amounts even water could be defined as a drug. (You can Google a self-inflicted disease called hyponatremia.) Abuse occurs when the substance is not taken for medical reasons, not as prescribed, or irresponsibly. Tolerance occurs when the same dose of the drug produces diminishing results. As such, larger and larger doses will be taken to get the original effects.

These substances affect the body's central nervous system (CNS), including the brain, brain stem, and spinal cord. They affect the person's eyesight and pupil size; heart (pulse and blood pressure); respiration rate; balance and coordination; motor skills; behavior; and decision-making and thought processes.

Dealing with Patrons with Mental Health Disorders

Substance abuse stages range from use to abuse, following this usual path (more slowly for alcohol and quite quickly for stimulant drugs and opiates):

- Experimentation
- Social use
- Regular use
- Daily preoccupation
- Dependency/addiction

People come into libraries in various stages of sobriety. The good news is you probably won't even notice if they are under the influence of drugs or alcohol. Some folks can control their use of various legal and illegal drugs, over-the-counter meds, prescriptions, or street goodies. The bad news is that many people, especially in the latter stages of their addictions, cannot control their behavior and you get to see and hear a lot of unique and interesting things. Alcoholics and stimulant drug users bring their own erratic and cyclical behavior issues to the library. They need to be managed in different ways than the opiate users, who tend not to be confrontational, at least when they are under the influence of their drug of choice.

When it comes to patrons and sobriety, your best tools are what you see and what you smell. The eyes are the window to the soul, and the nose knows. Your eyes should be looking at their eyes, for pupil size, eyelid bulge or droop, and redness. Most people who are not using stimulant drugs like cocaine or methamphetamine (relax, coffee is not that type of stimulant drug, even in the mass quantities some librarians consume) will have pupil sizes ranging from 3 millimeters to 6.5 millimeters in normal light. Opiate drug users who are under the influence will have pin dot pupils, from 1 to 3 millimeters, in normal light. Stimulant drug users will have blown out or dilated pupils from 7 to 10 millimeters. Red eyes can come from a variety of reasons: lack of sleep, allergies, or an infection. In our context, where we are assessing a patron's eyes for substance abuse, it's usually connected to marijuana use (red, irritated) or heavy alcohol use (glassy, red, bloodshot).

How do police and medical professionals know how big a drug user's pupils are? They use a card full of black dots of various millimeter sizes called a pupilometer. It's not that hard to see. Get into the habit of looking at people's pupils, and you will see some interesting size ranges.

Your nose should be smelling for three distinct odors on the person: alcohol, marijuana, and body odor (or sometimes all three). The reasons for the first, which you may smell simultaneously or separately, suggest alcohol use—which has its own set of cyclical, up/down, in control/out of control, angry/peaceful behaviors. The second odor—marijuana smoke—(and not all pot users smoke the flower; they vape it, or use edibles) will suggest compliance and complacency. Pot users are not often fighters. They may use the drug for pain control, sleep help, or to take the edge off their withdrawal from alcohol or street drugs. The third smell—body odor—may suggest depression, mental health issues, homelessness, or the most important, withdrawal from stimulant drugs.

Patrons who use meth (common) or cocaine (rare) will raise their body temperature dramatically, sweat a lot, not bathe or change their clothes regularly, especially when they are high or in withdrawal, and not care too much about personal hygiene. Not everyone who hasn't showered is a drug user, of course, but it is yet another behavioral warning sign for those who do.

Look at the "total patron": his or her overall appearance, pupil size, odors, balance and coordination, interactions, and hostility or cooperation. Use your intuition to size up the level of sobriety for patrons you encounter at work. Most of us know what it's like to have had a bit too much to drink, so we can often recognize the signs and symptoms of alcohol impairment. People under the influence of stimulant drugs tend to be aggressive and confrontational. People under the influence of depressant drugs tend to be more passive or even lethargic. People in withdrawal from either type of drug can be agitated and unpredictable. Be careful around anyone who seems out of control.

Consider that today, most paramedic responses for an unresponsive person down and under the age of thirty will be to give him or her Narcan because they suspect an opiate overdose. If they came across an older gentleman (like me) down on the ground they would break out the AED (automated external defibrillator) machine because they believe it's a heart attack. The national statistics for opiate drug overdoses suggest something like 135 to 175 people per day.[5] Paramedics are just playing the law of averages, as quickly as they can.

Speak to your bosses or coworkers about specific observations and medical or behavioral concerns. Share your observations with a coworker or boss to verify what you think you see if you're not sure. Get paramedics en route if you have any doubts that the person is in or will be in medical distress.

Keep in mind it could be a blood sugar issue with the person, which seems to mimic the symptoms of someone under the influence of alcohol. It's a useful question to ask, "Do you have a blood sugar issue today?" if you see slow movements, slurred words, stumbling, sweating, and incoherence. You may even get a slight whiff of the odor of what might be alcohol but could also be ketosis (sometimes called "fruity breath" because it smells like spoiled fruit).

DRUG EXPOSURE DANGERS

There is always the possibility of a needle stick any time a person has used a needle to inject drugs in the library stacks or in our restroom and then left it behind. The drugs of concern when it comes to library patrons who overdose and/or the residue they leave behind in our restrooms, stacks, shelves, book drops, lawns, and bushes is either heroin or fentanyl. Both are powders that are turned into liquids when the user adds water, heats the mixture, and injects it.

Dealing with Patrons with Mental Health Disorders

As a synthetic opiate, fentanyl is fatal to ingest in a dosage equal to about ten grains of sand (2 milligrams). Its deadlier cousin, carfentanil, is fatal to ingest at a dose about the size of two grains of sand (.02 milligrams). The good news is that even if you're exposed to these powders by just touching them, you're probably not going to feel the effects, since they don't enter through your skin. But, if you happen to inhale them or swallow them, or get a flake or two on an open cut, you could have a serious medical problem on your hands.

Opiate users with an overdose sometimes may have the needle still in their arm, leg, or between their toes. We need to treat them as a human hazmat situation, where there's a possibility of a drug exposure or a needle stick for anybody who comes in contact with them, including staff or paramedics who give them Narcan.

The issue we face in the library is that these people leave their drug paraphernalia—never their drugs—around after they have finished. As a long-time heroin user once told me, "We're very careful with our drugs. We're not very careful with our drug kits." This means we may find empty lighters; burned matches; tie-off ropes, cords, or belts; bloody bandages or rags; soda cans and spoons; and soggy cigarette filters (they draw the liquid heroin or fentanyl through the cotton filter, which has soaked up the drug, believing this is somehow "more hygienic"). Of course, the biggest risk factor item is a used or often broken-tipped syringe.

As such, our Rule of Thumb in the library is that we should treat all unknown or suspicious liquids (which could be heroin or PCP), solids (black or brown tar heroin, opiate pills, marijuana), or powders (cocaine, methamphetamine, heroin, synthetic opiates), or pills (Vicodin, Ecstasy) as if they could be instantly poisonous. This means if you encounter anything that looks like a potential hazmat (hazardous material), you need to stay clear of it, keep patrons and staff away from it, and notify trained facilities or maintenance personnel to remove it and clean around it. This person will need to dispose of it while wearing not just gloves, but a mask as well. (You can call the police to come and impound narcotics, but they may or may not respond, based on staffing and radio call volume issues.)

INTERACTING WITH NON-SOBER PATRONS

When in doubt about irrational people and their level of sobriety, stay clear of them and pay attention to your safety. Call the police if they're having behavior problems or they want to hurt themselves or others. Call paramedics if the person is having medical issues that seem severe enough that they need a medical evaluation. (This is most common when opiate users overdose and pass out in public places.)

Not all people under the influence of drugs or alcohol are violent, but many can become agitated if they feel provoked, frustrated, or prevented from doing something or from getting their way. Some of these people use their intoxication as their excuse for hurting someone or even themselves. They may have rapid mood swings, going from tears to threats to anger to apologies, all in a few minutes. Use simple language, ask simple questions, and speak in low tones. Keep your distance (no closer than ten or so feet away) and be ready to put barriers between you and the person (desks, carts, half-shelves, tables, chairs, etc.). Disengage if you feel threatened and wait in a safe location for the police to arrive.

Decide if the person you are dealing with can simply be asked, politely, to leave the facility, or if you need to call the police, or if his or her problem is medical. In some instances, the police may arrive and take the person to a mental health facility for an examination; in others, the fire department or EMTs may take the person to a hospital for treatment. While you don't always need to speak to your supervisor first as to which of these options to choose, it may help to have a brief group discussion as to the best choice.

Sometimes, you may have a good rapport, previous experience, or a good connection with a suspected drug or alcohol abuser. You may be able to talk to this person in a way that keeps him or her calm and relatively rational. In other situations, nothing you do or say will satisfy this person. Keep in mind that what might have worked well in the past (i.e., asking the person to leave) might suddenly become the triggering event for an argument or a fight now. Use your intuition and know when to talk and when to leave or get help.

Opiate addicts inside the library are most often found passed out in one of the chairs or at a table, or in the public restroom. From your vantage point and depending on your life experience being around people who use drugs or alcohol (or both, in heavy combinations), if it looks like they are high on something and are nonresponsive, first, send a coworker to call the paramedics and alert a supervisor, and second, watch them carefully until help arrives.

People who have slumped completely over from a heroin or opiate pill overdose will have difficulty breathing. If this happens, their hands and feet may develop a bluish tinge, which indicates cyanosis or a lack of blood flow and oxygen to their extremities. Often just moving them from a slumped-over position back up to a normal sitting position can improve their breathing rate by taking their body weight pressure off their lungs. If it really looks like they have stopped breathing, it's best to get a coworker to help get them out of their chair and lay them completely flat on the floor. If it looks like they are breathing on their own, you may want to roll them slightly onto their side so they don't aspirate if they vomit.

THE "NEW" METHAMPHETAMINE: LIBRARY PATRONS UNDER THE INFLUENCE OF A BAD DRUG

You've heard of "New Math"? How about "New Meth"?

This information comes from my drug abuse training colleague, Keith Graves, a retired detective and patrol sergeant from a Northern California police department. Keith holds a unique training certification; he's known as a DRE, or a drug recognition expert. He was the Drug Investigator of the Year for the California Narcotics Officers Association (where I'm also a member), so he knows his stuff.

Here are some quotes from a recent blog Keith wrote about the disturbing differences between new meth and old meth:

> You can't even call this methamphetamine anymore. The methamphetamine of today is made differently than it was just a few short years ago. With this change in manufacturing, there was a huge change in the way users reacted to this new meth and now methamphetamine is a major factor in police shootings. Simply put, methamphetamine is causing psychosis that is leading to paranoid behavior that leads to deadly interactions with law enforcement.[6]
>
> Methamphetamine is a powerful and highly addictive stimulant that can be smoked, snorted, or injected. Methamphetamine is now considered a serious public health threat due to its increased popularity and severe reactions to users. The drug is made in illegal labs in Mexico and then transported across the Mexico/US border. Methamphetamine is very potent and can be very addictive. In years past, methamphetamine was made with pseudoephedrine. To stop the manufacture of methamphetamine in the United States, the federal government clamped down on pseudoephedrine by restricting its sale. In a few short years, meth labs all but ceased to exist in the United States.
>
> However, Mexican Drug Trafficking Organizations (Cartels) started to make methamphetamine using phenyl-2-propanone ("P2P"). This is an old school method of making meth taken from the 1980s. Unfortunately for meth users, this "new" P2P manufacturing method was causing severe psychosis in meth users. This psychosis is often called meth psychosis.
>
> Methamphetamine psychosis is a mental health condition that can occur when someone uses methamphetamine. It is a type of psychosis, which is a mental health condition in which people have distorted thoughts and perceptions. People with methamphetamine psychosis may experience hallucinations, which are seeing things that are not real. They may also have a heightened sense of awareness and feel like they are in a state of constant danger.
>
> When you encounter someone that is experiencing meth psychosis, keep a social distance from him or her, about a 7 to 10-foot radius. You should also not deal with a person experiencing meth psychosis by yourself. Talk to the person in a calm and soft voice. A meth user hears a sound at a fast pace and a high pitch. A side effect of a meth high is a constant buzzing sound in the background of their ears and brain.
>
> Move in a deliberate manner. This will lessen the chances that the patron will misinterpret your actions. Keep your hands in sight. Because of the paranoia, your hands should be visible to the person. This does not put you at a disadvantage. If your hands are not visible, the patron might feel threatened and become violent.

Keep them talking. Silence can mean that the patron's paranoid thoughts have taken over and anyone in the area can become part of the meth user's paranoid delusions.[7]

Some closing thoughts from Keith Richards: "I'll drink anything that's available. If there ain't anything around, I don't drink. If I think, 'I can handle this better with a drink,' I'll take it. Compared to the other stuff I did, a drink is gnat's whiz."

NOTES

1. "Concept of Trauma and Guidance for a Trauma-Informed Approach," Substance Abuse and Mental Health Services Administration, July 2014, https://bit.ly/3iYtVq3.
2. December 13, 2016, https://www.scientificamerican.com/article/1-in-6-americans-takes-a-psychiatric-drug/.
3. https://www.incb.org/documents/Publications/AnnualReports/AR2021/Annual_Report/E_INCB_2021_1_eng.pdf. Page 24.
4. Cindy Grove, personal interview with the author, May 3, 2022, Rockport, Massachusetts.
5. https://www.cdc.gov/drugoverdose/epidemic/index.html.
6. February 13, 2022, https://gravesassociates.com/methamphetamine-is-a-major-factor-in-police-shootings/.
7. Ibid.

6

The Top Ten Most Challenging Patrons

Perhaps another name for this chapter might be, "How and Why to Talk about Tough Topics with Anyone" because it's not easy to talk with most patrons about their behavioral issues. Maybe you have better success than most, but we could probably count on one and a half hands the number of truly problematic patrons in your career who admitted their behavioral failings and complied with your first request, and you never had to ask them again.

We should ever only care about behavior when it comes to library patrons, not what they look like or any other physical or demographic factor. In Days of Old, when I was a fledgling library security consultant, both my instincts about human behavior on the streets and in and around the library caused me to refer to various challenging patrons as "Difficult." As in, their personalities were difficult, or their behavior was difficult to control, or interacting with them, especially on a regular basis, was difficult. At worst, "difficult" is a loaded word, and it's also a pejorative label. Some of my library leadership clients suggested I switch my use of that label to a descriptive phrase that's more accurate, less derogatory, and broader: Challenging Patrons.

In my defense, when I started teaching my library security training workshop back in 2000, "difficult" was the term a lot of library leaders and employees also used. I suspect their use of the term "difficult" to describe patron behaviors (and/or related personality traits, flaws, or obstacles) came out of the same sense of frustration that I have had in dealing with people who are occasionally not compliant, sometimes uncooperative, and often just headstrong, fixed, entitled, and opinionated. I see less of the term now, but when I encounter it, it reminds me that, with some exceptions, most people who we might see as difficult are mostly challenging, meaning they have internal goals or solutions that are hidden from us. As always, my concept of the "Essential Eight" is the same for every patron you encounter: firm, fair, consistent, legal, assertive, empathic, patient, and reasonable. Not surprisingly, these eight are also the traits of skilled listeners, which every library employee needs to be.

"COACHING UP" THE CHALLENGING TEN (WHO CAN OCCUPY 80 PERCENT TO 95 PERCENT OF YOUR TIME)

For some situations and library locations, that 80–20 difficulty number zooms up to 95 percent of problems tending to be caused by 5 percent of the patrons. If you're lucky in your library, that ratio may go down as far as 99 percent who are reasonable, affable, cooperative, and supportive patrons and only 1 percent who are problematic. In some libraries, the only problem patron is "that guy" who comes in and stirs things up or "that lady" who makes the staff and the supervisors cringe when she comes through the door.

Successful patron behavior management means we may have to spend a lot of time "coaching up" that 5 to 20 percent group who show up so often in our Security Incident Reports, security guard or police officer discussions, supervisor interventions, and staff meetings. The technical phrase for "coaching up" challenging patrons might be to say, "We will attempt to apply fair, reasonable, and consistent behavioral improvement or behavioral management techniques, with the goal of gaining the patron's compliance, so that he or she makes the changes we would appreciate seeing." Whew! Quite a mouthful.

I have a deep background in customer service training, having learned at the feet of my father, Dr. Karl Albrecht, whose 1985 book, *Service America! Doing Business in the New Economy*, sold 750,000 copies. I wrote my own book on service skills for employees and leaders, and after teaching many programs, especially to public-sector employees, I came to a realization about our goals with our customers. Should our goal in the library be that every patron leaves thrilled with the experience and raving to others about the level of service he or she received? That's certainly attainable and it would be fun if they all left with a spring in their steps, but it's not always realistic. Despite your absolute best efforts, some patrons will just shrug at you and wander away after you spent two hours helping them on the internet. Take heart that you did your very best. Should our goal be that we did the bare minimum for them and they left feeling underserved from the experience? No. That's not what we're hired to do, and that will not meet their expectations. In truth, our service goal with all of our patrons is that they leave our library "satisfied that we did our best for them and they received the level of service they expected." It's their expectations that count. In this country, people have a very high expectation that they will be just as well served by a retail business as by a public-sector business.

As you consider how my list of Ten Challenging Patrons compares to yours, make it your goal to do your very best with everyone and move on, knowing you did. We can't pick our patrons and we can't solve all of their problems, but for that brief or long span that we connect, we will give it our max effort.

Before I get into the who, with challenging patrons, let's talk about the how and the why. When it comes to "coaching up" problematic patrons, maybe it's time to try something called the "Shamu Method."

To write her book, *What Shamu Taught Me about Life, Love, and Marriage: Lessons for People from Animals and Their Trainers* (2008), Amy Sutherland spent a year visiting an animal training center in California, watching trainers use various techniques to train a variety of animals ranging from the exotic (camels and dolphins) to the standard (dogs, cats, and birds). As she put it, she had a fascinating time observing the trainers as they went about "teaching hyenas to pirouette on command, cougars to offer their paws for a nail clipping, and baboons to ride a skateboard."[1]

In her book, Sutherland wrote about a useful training tool that works for humans and animals, based on a behavioral modification concept known as "extinction." In an article found on the Verywell Mind website, author Kendra Cherry defines this concept by saying, "In psychology, extinction refers to the gradual weakening of a conditioned response that results in the behavior decreasing or disappearing. In other words, the conditioned behavior eventually stops."[2] And it all has to do with praising what we like and ignoring what we don't.

It's a useful idea for understanding how humans and animals learn, and more accurately, how we unintentionally reinforce negative behaviors with our usual responses of anger, punishment, ridicule, shaming, and frustration. Here, we don't focus on the negative outcome—with humans, let's call it a failure to do a more positive behavior or the continuation of a negative behavior, even harder and faster. Instead, we ignore the behavior completely; in effect, we "extinguish" it and let it "go extinct." Calling it out just gives it more energy, adding more fuel to a repetitive fire. Even bad attention is still attention.

Instead, we use praise when the person (or your dog or cat, or elephant, if you have the room for one) does what we want them to do, even just a little bit and only for a moment. This concept builds on the idea that people and animals dislike verbal abuse and especially hate physical punishment. Humans and especially children respond to verbal praise—"Great job! Thanks for helping me out!" and physical rewards (in the pre-COVID days, a hug if they want one, a pat on the back, a pay raise). For domesticated animals, praise is about food first (we give Tabby a kitty treat when she doesn't tear up the couch and uses the new scratching post instead) and physical contact second (petting, ear scratching, chin rubs). For wild animals (and my Pug), it's always about the food.

Perhaps this idea is best illustrated by a common and tedious example experienced by every parent of a two-year-old. You take your kid with you to the grocery store, and once you reach the cereal aisle, his or her eyes light up when he or she sees the usual assortment of Double Chocolate Frosted Sugar Bombs.

The Top Ten Most Challenging Patrons

Thus begins a typical pattern where he or she asks for more and more different kinds of not-so-healthy cereals and you, as the increasingly exasperated parent, go from "No!" to "I said, NO!" in fairly short order. This is often followed by, "I'm not going to tell you again!," whereupon you say it again one minute later, and then finally give in to get what we all want, Peace in the Valley. Soon your child is drying his or her tears, holding a box of Sweet Victory, and you feel manipulated and now dread the short walk over to the Big Bag of Candies Aisle, where the process beings anew.

Using the extinction concept, the parent says, "No cereal today," as soon as he or she reaches the cereal aisle with their child. No matter how loudly the child asks, screams, cries, falls on the floor, and repeats the cycle, the parent should not make eye contact, just finish getting what he or she needs, and move with the kid to the next aisle. No verbal interaction, no angry looks, no shouting, no Big Scene. The moment the child does something positive, the parent should say, "Thanks for handing me the aluminum foil. I really like it when you help me."

The bad news is this approach requires something many parents have in short supply: patience to let the tool work. My daughter—thirty now but once a Mighty Terror at the grocery store—would get me nearly every time to say those fatal words, "Okay! I'll get you the box of Assorted Teeth Rotteners, if you promise to stop crying/complaining/asking. But only this one time!" Of course, she won by wearing Dad down, which meant the cycle would repeat at the toy store, prom dress store, car dealership, and so on.

For this process to work, it requires the patience to suppress your usual emotions to scold the child or attempt to comfort them once the tears start. Kids around the planet know that if they cry hard and long enough and the parent gives in every time to whatever they want, the tool works and brilliantly at that. Giving in once makes you set the Behavioral Training Clock back to Minute Zero. Extinction is not easy, and it is not fast; however, it does work, given time, patience, and consistency of method.

As another part of extinction, Amy Sutherland wrote in her book how the trainers she saw defined it: "I followed the students to SeaWorld San Diego, where a dolphin trainer introduced me to least reinforcing syndrome (L.R.S.). When a dolphin does something wrong, the trainer doesn't respond in any way. He stands still for a few beats, careful not to look at the dolphin, and then returns to work. The idea is that any response, positive or negative, fuels a behavior. If a behavior provokes no response, it typically dies away."[3]

Growing up in San Diego, California, with Sea World nearby, I saw this training process play out many times. When Shamu the Orca did a trick correctly, it got a fish (Shamu got a lot of fish; he/she weighs four to six tons) and a playful rub on its slippery snout. When Shamu did not do the trick correctly or even refused to do it, the trainer broke eye contact, did something else, and came back to try again. Successful trick: fish, rubs, eye contact, and moving on.

You cannot punish a killer whale, an elephant, or a camel. You cannot punish people and have them thank you for it. You can use lots of praise and rewards, even when the positive change is slight. Good behavior builds to more good behavior; it's human and animal nature because we are all hedonists, searching for pleasure and avoiding pain.

How about we try this in the library environment? Every time we use a frustrated or condescending tone to lecture problematic patrons about our Code of Conduct or our rules and policies about behavior, we add energy to that negative behavior. What about another approach, where we ignore the bad things they do until the moment they do the right thing, and then we catch them doing it right and thank them for it?

Obviously, safety trumps behavior modification. If a patron is doing something illegal, threatening, dangerous, or violent, we don't ignore it in the hopes they will do something good later on.

Let's try "coaching this patron up" with the Shamu/extinction method:

A patron tosses a book onto the table and it misses and hits the floor. He looks at you for a moment. You pick it up and place it on the reshelving cart without making eye contact with him or saying a word. He heads out the door. The next day, he does it again and you do it again, without addressing his negative behavior. On the third day, he places the book on the table and you say, "Are you all done with that book? [You check the title.] That looks like an interesting subject. Thanks for putting it there. I'll put it in my reshelving cart in case you need it again before I put it back."

Might it be possible that one day, fairly soon or a month from now, he places it on the reshelving cart for you? It can't hurt to try the Shamu/Extinction Method on patrons who you want to be more compliant with our rules. Start with small examples and work up to the Big Behavioral Stuff. Take your Patience Pills and talk as a staff as to how you can all do the same technique as a group, so the patron sees a consistent message from all of you.

THE LIST

I compiled this collection of Ten Challenging Patrons based on input I've received from library directors, managers, supervisors, and full- and part-time staffers (and even a few patrons who have flagged me down as I've wandered through or sat for hours and even days in various libraries in my security consulting capacity). You'll notice that for some categories I've included the opposite patron—for example, the patron who steals versus the patron who leaves his or her stuff to be stolen. The first can be concerning, to be sure; the second can be maddening.

As with all things in Library Life—as we strive to reach my Perfect Library World—all of what you read here about patron behaviors will get my usual measures: "What is this person's impact on the business? Is this a behavioral concern I or we need to address because it's hurting the safe and secure operation of our library?" The answers to those questions are easy to derive when they are a clear yes or an unhesitating no. Much of human behavior, however, falls into the middle category of "well, it depends." (This is also a good answer when certain library security consultants named Steve are puzzled as to the best answer of how to deal with really problematic patron behaviors.)

Context is always a crucial key; what bothers you doesn't seem to bother your coworker. What irritates your boss doesn't bother you. What bothers a nearby patron, who seems a tad hypersensitive or easily offended, may be just an ordinary Tuesday for you, and so forth.

It can help to look at the bigger picture with some of these patrons—especially those you consider your "Frequent Fliers" and not in a fun way. Do they replicate these behaviors on a day in/day out, regular basis, or only once in a while? Do you get many complaints from patrons or only a few? What does your intuition say when you ask yourself this sort of qualifying question: "Would this same behavior, by this same person be tolerated at Starbucks or McDonald's or the local park?" If your answer is "no," then there you go. If your answer is "yes," then move on to your other duties as assigned. If your answer is "maybe," then ask yourself, "If I address this now, can I prevent it from escalating? Or will it get worse because I am addressing it?" (For some people, even negative attention is good attention.) Will this become an issue I have to go to my supervisor for help? Is there a more qualified person (coworker or boss) or who has better alignment than I that I I should get?"

Considering that I have already covered harassing patrons, and patrons experiencing homelessness, mental health issues, and drug/alcohol use in previous chapters, I won't repeat myself here. You'll note that I have taken a deeper dive into some of these patrons' behaviors, not only because their behavior interests me but also because they may be a bit outside the norm of what you usually see.

You'll note some similarities in my suggested approaches with many of these patrons: using the "best fit" alignment for them; showing patience; demonstrating empathy; letting them vent, with validation; listening with skill; creating better boundaries with them; following your Code of Conduct, and enforcing consequences.

THE LONELY, NEEDY PATRON

This patron's biggest issue is he or she can take up a lot of your time. This person may be lonely, needy, and patiently seeking social connections or lonely, needy, and impatient with you. Sometimes, they think the world revolves around them and they may not realize you have other duties or other patrons to serve. One approach is to partner them up with another like-minded patron who shares their interests. Or introduce them to programs or subjects you sense might be a good fit for them. It's okay not to feel guilty about "not helping them enough." Sometimes the best you can do is all you can do.

THE TECHNOLOGICALLY CONFUSED PATRON

This patron can go in two directions: he or she really doesn't know or can't remember how to operate the PC, laptop, or tablet you just finished explaining yesterday, or they just like having you do things for them, over and over again. It's easy to lose patience with this person.

There is a segment of the population, often elderly, that thinks or says some version of, "I don't have the energy, patience, desire, or motivation to learn new things, especially technology things, so I'll just play passive and have others use them for me." This can lead you to demonstrate, over and over again, even the simplest operations for the various devices in your library. Some staffers have created cheat sheets, templates, laminated cards, and even pages of photos to help their patrons figure out what they need to do to be more self-sufficient. This requires effort and patience. It can be frustrating when patrons don't seem to listen, retain, or memorize what they need to do every time they want to log on, access various library services, or get on the internet. One of my friends told me about his dog, who was always found sleeping on the couch. He told his dog to get off the couch every single day for ten straight years before one day, he came home and the dog was not sleeping on the couch. It can be a little like that with some technologically resistant or tech-phobic patrons.

THE STARING PATRON

This issue really, really annoys a lot of female library employees, who talk with me about it regularly. There are a lot of reasons for this kind of behavior from a patron, and many staffers take it to mean a sexual reason at worst ("he's undressing me with his eyes!"), or it's just done to make them feel uncomfortable, even if the person has innocent motives. Saying, "Don't take it personally" sounds like a dismissive answer, but it may not go deeper than that with some patrons, who lack social skills, are just bored and don't know where else to look, or may be on the autism spectrum and, if so, may not have a caregiver in the library. For some men, it's a nervous habit, a tic, an uncontrollable behavior. It's often hard to know what is the person's motive for doing it and it may continue, even if you tell him directly to stop.

My sense for this particular issue is that you need to be "assertively polite" (a phrase you may see often in and around this chapter) and say, "It seems like you're staring at me. If so, I need you to stop. Thank you." I see too many examples where employees apologize while asking the patron to stop doing something—for example, "Could you please . . .?" Or "I'm sorry, but could you . . ." That's not the best approach. Say what you want to say, without qualifiers or restrictions.

The patron's reaction to your request may be any of the following: surprise, indignation, embarrassment, shock, an apology, a denial, or a shrug. Be ready for any of these, and if your request doesn't work, do it again the next time it happens. After you reach your limit, speak to your supervisor about getting his or her help for the issue. As you will see in our later discussion concerning patrons on the autism spectrum, the staring habit may be out of his control.

THE TRIPLE-E PATRONS (ENTITLED, ECCENTRIC, EXASPERATING) WHO IGNORE OUR RULES

Here, we get three patrons for the price of one! If you work on the front line of daily patron interactions at your library, it's easy to go home tired. Having what is defined as a "high human contact" job means that you can get weary of dealing with people all day, at the counter, over the phone, and on the floor. This is especially true if—like me—you're an introvert (writer-trainer) trapped in an extrovert's profession (customer service). Sometimes it's a struggle to get through the day without feeling or getting impatient with the wide range of people you encounter in a long day.

It's important to follow good self-care protocols, including taking your breaks, eating healthy snacks or lunches, getting some exercise before or after work or as part of your breaks, and getting good sleep. Other times, when your interactions with patrons reach the limits of your patience, empathy, and concern, it's good to remember that good service is a "we issue" not just a "me issue." It's perfectly acceptable and even advisable to get help from coworkers or bosses if you're having difficulty communicating or serving certain patrons.

Part of that help can take the form of group discussions, formal or informal staff meetings, one-on-one discussions with colleagues or your boss, and training meetings designed to come up with strategies to help serve and communicate with our most challenging patrons. These meetings can take the form of role-plays, rehashing common scenarios, talking about past experiences that didn't work out so well, and using group synergy to create better, different approaches the next time you see such patrons.

Every library has its share of Frequent Fliers, those patrons who come in regularly enough to demonstrate behavioral habits, good and not-so-good. While it's not useful or fair to label people, we can define three types or archetypes of patron behavior that can be called the Triple E Group: Entitled, Eccentric, and Exasperating. See if some of these folks sound familiar, as part of your workday encounters:

THE ENTITLED PATRON

This is the person whose favorite phrase appears to be: "I pay your salary!" whether he or she says it out loud or not. As an example, you could work with this patron for two hours on the internet, helping with a resume or multiple job applications, and at the end of all that hear no version of "thank you." Sometimes they just wander off, believing perhaps that you owe them all that effort without any appreciation because that's what you're being paid to do. They can be dismissive if you don't help right away. They ignore our rules, refuse to cooperate, and have no patience for waiting for others to get help first. They use verbal or physical intimidations, aggressive behaviors, or even bullying. They can be sarcastic, rude, and demeaning in conversations. This seems to work for them in other life encounters—at the bank, the restaurant, and the Department of Motor Vehicles. They often have low self-esteem, which they mask with bullying and bravado.

THE ECCENTRIC PATRON

This patron takes many forms, from the town's richest citizen who intentionally dresses in filthy rags (just to see how people treat him), to a person who we later discover had undiagnosed mental health or dementia issues, to the person who is just a free spirit and dresses and acts in ways that are designed to draw attention from the rest of the people they encounter in their daily walkabout. Other behaviors include farting, nonsensical conversations, talking to himself or herself, hygiene issues, or walking around with cash money falling out of their pockets. They may not dress like it, but they could even be the richest person in town. They may come in alone or with a caregiver or family member. Most are just harmless. Their biggest sin is the attention-getting time drain and the occasional complaint from another patron that they have wandered over and taken a book off the table that the patron who is sitting there was just about to read.

"Eccentricity is in the eye of the employee," meaning what bothers, amazes, or offends one staffer doesn't have much of an effect on another. It's all about tolerance, patience, and perception. As one perfect example of a completely lovable eccentric, search Amazon Prime for the 1950 Jimmy Stewart movie *Harvey*. Watch that adorable film and think about who might be just like him in your library.

THE EXASPERATING PATRON

These are the people who make you cringe inwardly when they enter your library. There are lots (and lots) of different versions of this patron, ranging from rude teenagers to rude senior citizens; overly chatty patrons who monopolize your time and energy and won't let you serve others; the patron with a thousand questions; the patron who stares at you all day; the patron with chronic hygiene problems; the one who likes to argue with you and even debate with other patrons, just to argue; the patron who hogs "their" internet PC all day and night; or the patron who consistently violates the small rules of polite society or the rules of good library behavior to the point where you and your colleagues and bosses are seriously frustrated with him or her.

These people don't seem to learn from previous encounters and choose not to remember, agree to, or follow our behavioral rules or Codes of Conduct. Exasperation is in the eye of the beholder; what bothers you may not bother your coworker and vice versa. Most of these people can be harmless, but they also can be a conversational and operational time drain for you if you're not prepared to create better boundaries with how you serve them. It's okay to say, "I need to go and do other parts of my job," instead of just saying, "I need to go help other patrons."

The secrets to working with, serving, and minimizing the negative impact of these "Triple E" patron types are easy to say and more challenging to do. But in the spirit of future success, give these service tools a try; they work:

- Do the best you can. (All you can do is your job, to the best of your efforts.)
- Be patient, empathic, and neutral. (Don't argue, let them push your hot buttons, or let them rile you up.)
- Don't take their personalities personally. (It's them, not you.)
- Be firm, fair, reasonable, assertive, and consistent with them. (Set a professional service standard and stick with it.)
- Praise them when they comply or demonstrate even a little patience themselves. (Kill them with kindness, assert your assertiveness, and practice professionalism.)
- Don't take them home inside your head. (Leave work, and the tough conversations you had, at work.)

THE PATRON WHO PURPOSELY DISPLAYS PORNOGRAPHY

We can call this type of patron "The Unabashed Pornography Enthusiast" because that seems to be all he wants to look at. Even on their own device, tablet, phone, and despite repeated warnings from you and your colleagues, they continue.

Serious question: Why do men watch porn in the library, a public environment? I know why men and women watch porn. (Having never seen any myself, I've heard there is a lot of it on this place called "the internet.") What I don't understand is why some men choose to watch porn in front of others. At the library. They rarely try to hide their intentions or their actions. Is it simply because they like being provocative, immature, and intrusive? Yes. They do it because they can. They enjoy the thrill, the attention, being provocative, annoying others, and pushing boundaries in a public place. They don't have internet access. They don't own a cell phone, tablet, or laptop. They can't watch it at their home or workplace. They are chronologically and sexually immature. They have an addictive personality, even with consequences of being kicked off your internet or banned from the library. They may have a mental illness, a paraphilia, an obsessive-compulsive disorder, or a sex addiction, or they are just narcissistic enough to enjoy even negative attention.

Follow your Code of Conduct and internet use policies, and be assertive as you tell this patron to comply or leave. This patron may even sexually expose himself (a crime) and deny it ever happened. Your response: "Let's take a look at the security camera video, shall we? Still time to change your version of the events before I call the police."

THE TWEENAGED / PROBLEM STUDENT / YOUNG BULLY PATRON

I love my adult daughter more than breathing. But when she was between twelve and about sixteen, she was a holy terror. This is a tough age for a lot of kids—a powerful collision of puberty, hormones, immaturity, anti-authority feelings, peer pressure, and an intense desire not to be embarrassed in front of their peers by other kids or adults. Library staffers tell me their most challenging patrons—after mentally ill and/or inebriated homeless people—are tweenagers, teenagers, and students. These kids can work in groups to make the library a loud, disruptive, even fearful place, as they bully other kids, bother adults, and disobey and insult staff. Many older library patrons avoid the building during those witching hours from 2 p.m. to 5 p.m., when the nearby junior high or high school has let out and some of the kids are just a handful and a half.

It's easy for some library employees to lose patience with some kids who are loud and disrespectful in the library because they forget They Are Kids. Feeling their oats is in their DNA. Smarting off to adults goes back to our cave days; it just is what it is. Library leaders and staffers I've talked with over the years have offered some unique ideas to get better compliance with younger patrons. Consider these outside-the-box (OTB) solutions:

Hire willing students to work as interns, so they can help with the behavioral issues of their peers (and see how the shoe fits on the other foot); set up student zones in parts of the library where they are allowed to congregate and be noisy for a span of allotted time; ask willing students to help you set up peer support teams, to go around the library and talk things out with problematic students; create a reward program and incentives for kids who follow the library rules. Talk with your young adult and children's librarians to get their advice as well.

What kind of security help might we be able to get from our nearby schools? This starts with library leaders meeting with school leaders, both at the district superintendent's level and with the principals and vice principals, counselors, and the school security staff. That's a good time to talk about what "we" (the library and the school, in some loose or formal partnership) can do to keep the library safe and productive, by talking about student (and parent) educational opportunities on "good library behavior." Can we mutually develop rules of library conduct that can get sent out to parents and are supported by the school campuses?

If the nearby school has a police or sheriff's sworn representative who works as the school resource officer (SRO), can the library leaders also set a meeting with them to talk about expectations and support?

THE ANGRY PARENT PATRON

A typical scenario is when one or more angry parents come into the library, with their child in tow, to complain about something that happened (the day before, or when you were off work, or involving another staffer, who is not here today). The situation often involves an issue where their child was mistreated by another kid, a staff member, or another patron; bullied; or kicked out, even for being "extra quiet." As is often true with parent-teacher meetings, this parent may actually know his or her child is not an angel and may have even done what was alleged. But even the most reasonable parent will still want "justice" on behalf of his or her child.

Your approach is empathic listening, without letting any judgment leak out of your tone or body language. The other key is to separate the parties if you can. If two parents come in with their child, ask politely if you can speak with just one parent, off to the side, while the other waits with the kiddo. If they both insist on speaking, at least politely ask if they can both speak to you alone, while the child waits within eyesight. The reason for this separation is simple: so you don't get overwhelmed by too many people talking all at once. Listen carefully and don't throw yourself or a colleague down by saying, "Well, I wasn't here yesterday and I didn't talk with my coworker, who isn't here either, so I don't know who to believe." Instead, say, "I hear your frustration. I know I'd want my child or someone in my family treated well during their time here. Let me see if I can find out what happened. Can you give me a few minutes?" At that point, you can talk with other coworkers or bosses, review any Security Incident Reports, speak with your security officer, and try to get some verification before you return.

Keep in mind that the parents know exactly what kind of kid they have and how he or she usually acts in public. They are merely trying to get their story told and heard. Be polite and patient, but if no coworker in the library did anything wrong, don't apologize for the actions they took.

THE ELDERLY, PHYSICALLY DISABLED, DEPENDENT ADULT, OR DEVELOPMENTALLY DISABLED PATRON; OR AN ABUSER OF THOSE PATRONS

From a legal perspective, the law often defines senior citizens as people over the age of sixty or sixty-five and dependent adults as those people eighteen or over who have a physical or psychological disability and are unable to care for themselves. Other patrons of all ages may have disabilities—visible or not—which make them vulnerable to abuse by others, including their own family members or people hired to care for them. Because of these vulnerabilities, all states have laws that dictate what is a "mandated reporter" when it comes to reporting physical, emotional, or financial abuse, or neglect or abandonment of this sensitive population. This often includes library employees, who can be mandated reporters for the elderly, dependent adults, and children, all of whom they see as they work. These reports are most often made to social service agencies—Child Protective Services (CPS) for kids seventeen and under or Adult Protective Services (APS)—or to local law enforcement.

Library employees are likely to see the "caregivers" (and I put that term in quotes because they are not giving much care or are hurting these people) leave an elderly person or a disabled person in a corner of the library while they leave for three hours to get lunch or run errands. They may abandon someone they're supposed to care for in the library with no access to water or the restroom. You may see emotional or physical abuse by a "caregiver," who screams at or hits the person. You may see the elderly or disabled person is quite fearful of their "caregiver" and is afraid to be around him or her or go home with that person. These are all examples of elder or dependent adult abuse, and they need to be reported to APS as soon as it is safe for you to do so.

Just like with reporting child abuse to CPS, which many librarians already know how and why to do, calling APS requires you to be what I define as a "professional witness." This means you take careful note of the facts as you see them, including who did what to whom, what was said, when and where the incident took place, and any other details (e.g., license plates, cars, clothing descriptions, names, addresses, nicknames, etc.) that can be useful for the CPS or APS hotline folks who will be assigning these cases to social workers for an investigation.

THE PATRON WHO HOGS THE INTERNET

"That's *my* machine," says the out-of-breath patron, after he has dashed from the front door to the internet area, right at opening time. These patrons have an odd territoriality, aggressiveness, anger, anxiety, or even an obsessive-compulsiveness about quasi-ownership, cleanliness, and their space around others when it comes to "my desk, chair, personal computer, keyboard, mouse, table, and pen."

They can become confrontational when other patrons intrude on their space and their stuff. I have seen arguments and even fights in libraries over the exact same two internet computers. (Perhaps these patrons think they have certain magical powers.) These patrons have a number of eccentric habits. They can be curmudgeonly, have a brittle personality, challenge others (including you), and are often hypersensitive to being told what to do. One of the main problems of letting them declare ownership of a PC or their spot in your internet lineup is that it's hard to dethrone them once this habit has become ingrained. It's best to not allow this to happen at all and give all patrons access to any machine. You may have to have this conversation more than once, and they won't want to hear it. Stand your ground and be assertive. The library and its equipment is for everyone, and we don't play machine favorites here. These patrons need to share and cooperate or risk losing their internet privileges by arguing too much.

THE PATRON WHO PROTESTS ABOUT BOOKS OR OTHER CONTENT

Certain citizens in your communities have wanted to ban various books from libraries since the publication of Twain's *Huckleberry Finn*. These days, some people want libraries to remove books, magazines, young adult novels, DVDs, music, and even video games that they deem offensive. (As one library employee once told me with a smile, "When I ask these people if they have read the book or viewed the DVD that they are complaining about, a surprising number of times their answer is no. They are either offended by the title or someone told them to be offended about the material.")

For help in this area, I have called upon a library training colleague, Barry Trott, MSLS. He is an adult services consultant in the Library Development and Networking Division for the Library of Virginia. Here are his suggestions for managing the outcry and expectations of these patrons:[4]

- Be prepared before the challenge comes. Challenges to materials will come from all sides, even unexpected people/groups. Don't develop policy and procedures on the fly.
- Develop a set of policies and procedures on how a patron with a complaint should proceed.
- Solve the problem at the lowest level possible is best. Often frontline staff can avert a bigger problem simply by listening, but they need to be trained.
- Notify the library director when a complaint is made, even if it seems that it was resolved at the time it was made. Don't let your boss be surprised.

When a user has a complaint about content, do the following:

- Listen and empathize, but don't try to defend the item. It's not an educable moment. Don't make any promises or commitments too early.
- Say something like, "I'm sorry that this item/book/DVD was not to your liking. Let me help you find something that you might enjoy."
- Try to resolve by listening—a lot of times that is what they want—someone to listen to their concerns.
- Get their contact information if they persist and let them know that someone from the next level (department head, collection librarian, etc.) will reach out to them. That person will start the listening process over again, by phone or in person.
- Offer a formal Request for Reconsideration if the above does not solve the concern.

Once a formal request has been made, the complainant will receive a formal response from the director, department head, collection librarian, or other upper-level staff. This might include a reiteration of the library's commitment to providing materials for all members of the community, the library's commitment to intellectual freedom and the freedom to read, the library's collection policy, reviews of the item in question, circulation information that supports the community interest in the item, awards or other recognitions of the merit of the item, and any other appropriate information.

From there, the complaint may move to the library director, and if the library's procedures recommend to the library's governing body (library board, local government, etc.).

Barry suggests going to the American Library Association (ALA) website for their "tool kit" on this issue as well: https://www.ala.org/tools/challenge support/selectionpolicytoolkit.

TWO SPECIAL CIRCUMSTANCES: THE AUTISTIC PATRON AND THE PATRON WHO STEALS

THE AUTISTIC PATRON

Helping library patrons with autism starts with understanding. Dr. Jim Wining, a Missouri-based pastor and business leader, has two autistic sons. He has worked with this issue as a parent and as an advocate in the autism community for nearly four decades. He has graciously provided me with several important tools to help library staff interact with and serve autistic persons (APs).[5] He starts by discussing certain "triggers" in the library for autistic patrons, which may or may not lead to what is commonly referred to as a behavioral "meltdown."

Librarians—Staff should not raise their voices much above a whisper. The AP knows the voice level of a library probably better than the librarian, so if the librarian is unable to communicate with the AP, immediately seek additional support and avoid repeating instructions or directions. Always be prepared for confinement even if the person's guardian is present.

Bright lights—These should be avoided as autistic persons may react either catatonically or violently.

Touch—If advised of germ possibilities on books, the AP will neither open a book nor be in an area with the books.

Smell—Extreme odors, like disinfectants, may result in screaming or a near meltdown.

Directions—Try to avoid the "no" command. Go around it. If the AP asks for a book and it is checked out, answer this way, "The book will be available on [a future date]." Try to avoid saying words of rejection such as, "The book is checked out and not available."

Restrooms—This can be a source of extreme reaction including demands of cleanliness to disrupting the cleanliness of the restrooms. Try to recommend bathrooms with multiple stalls rather than single rooms with private locking doors.

"Meltdown"—This is a last-ditch effort by the AP to defend against a sensory attack, physical confrontation, and/or emotional event. A meltdown can include screaming, yelling, throwing objects, pounding his or her head against the wall, tearing flesh from his or her body, and other physical and nonphysical reactions to a perceived challenge.

Confinement—This is a step taken by two or more people to restrict the actions of an AP during a time of meltdown. The action involves forming a circle around the AP with your body and arms extended. Do not physically contact the AP but be prepared to be struck and to repel the attack. Do not administer physical restraint. The typical meltdown usually lasts three to five minutes, but when the AP is aggravated (or for some other unknown reason), it can last up to thirty minutes. Eliminate public contact around the meltdown area and seek the guardian's advice or public service including fire and police personnel. Firefighters or paramedics are usually better trained than police to handle such matters.

Social distancing—Space is your ally. The six-foot rule is perfect for seating, standing, and general movement in the library. Remember APs always have difficulty with socialization.

Checking out materials—Don't worry about eye contact but be careful not to take items from an AP. Let the AP voluntarily hand you the book or CD. Ask him or her for his or her library card or the guardian's card. If the AP has reached the Circulation Desk without a card, very calmly say, "The items will be right here in a visible, designated place and will be checked out to you when your card is presented." Be careful to itemize these items especially if they are "no check-out items" as they could likely disappear. If the guardian is not present, send someone to find him or her.

Leaving with materials without checking them out—If the AP is leaving with unauthorized material, immediately contact the guardian. If the guardian has left the library and is outside, motion to him or her for assistance. Do not follow the AP.

AP restrictions—APs should not be allowed to be in the library if he or she is required to have a guardian for life decisions, including health and welfare matters. If the AP has, in your best estimation, "diminished authority," a guardian must be present at all times. Seek help from a library supervisor to take the course of action mentioned above.

Violence—Physical or verbal conflict can occur instantly, without an apparent warning. For an AP, more frequently than not verbal conflict results in self-inflicted physical violence to the AP, not the perceived attacking party. If confinement fails within a five-minute period or the violence escalates, withdraw and call for police, paramedics, or firefighter help. Always keep the public away from the AP.

Drinking fountains and refreshments—Public drinking services are potential sites for a physical disruption and should be avoided. Limiting refreshments to water only is recommended. Other eating, drinking, or chewing items can be distracting to the AP and are a source of "fairness complaints," which can escalate into a situation.

Admission to the library—You must be aware at all times of an AP in the library. Therefore, require guests providing guardian services to notify staff upon entering. Jim Wining strongly recommends that guardians should be restricted to not more than three APs at a time. Look out for large numbers of group home members—five to ten APs with only one or two guardians. This is a high-risk situation that could trigger multiple meltdowns at a time.

Parking lot—If possible, have someone regularly check the parking lot for AP patrons. If you see an AP having problems in the parking lot, don't let him or her into the library. Meet the guardians at the main door and discuss their visit before anyone enters. You may want to postpone their visit, restrict their numbers, or only allow certain APs who are not in apparent danger. All library staff needs to monitor for behavioral concerns.

Safety first—If a meltdown occurs, contain the incident, decide if you need to evacuate the area, and then decide if you need to call your public safety professionals.

THE PATRON WHO STEALS / THE PATRON WHO LEAVES STUFF TO GET STOLEN

People steal things from the library for a variety of reasons, mostly selfish ones. It could be young kids who don't realize what they are doing is wrong. It could be teenagers, who get urged on by their friends to take something. Peer pressure, as we know, can be a big driver of bad behavior.

Some people will steal from the library because they need to pawn, sell, or trade the item for food because they are hungry. Some people steal from the library and trade what they got for drugs or alcohol, to feed their addictions. And some people steal from the library just because that's what they do; they steal from stores, homes, businesses, and cars. We call these people professional thieves; it's how they spend their days and nights, until they are arrested and convicted.

The list of things that can get stolen from the library is a long one: rare and regular books; Genealogy Room materials; library training room fixtures like projectors, speakers, or flat-screen TVs; DVDs and rentable DVD players; game consoles and video games; laptops, tablets, or smartphones that belong to the library (or even library employees) or to patrons; purses, backpacks, wallets, checkbooks, jewelry, cash, coins, and even expensive jackets and clothing belonging to patrons or staffers. I recall several cases where thieves stole from the community charity jars that were positioned at the Circulation Desk or near the library exit doors.

The law often defines theft in three categories: petty theft, grand theft, and burglary. Petty theft is usually valued at a dollar figure under a certain amount. Grand theft is charged for an amount stolen above the petty theft threshold.

Some states use their Penal Code statutes to set petty theft at under $1,000, others under $500, and still others at under $300. In some agriculture-oriented states, stealing avocados or livestock is always a felony. In many states, felony theft is usually what's called a "wobbler," meaning it "wobbles" between a state prison–felony punishment or a county jail–misdemeanor punishment, depending on the amount, the defendant's criminal history, and the circumstances.

Burglary is often defined as entering a dwelling with the intent to commit theft or any felony. By this definition, a thief could be charged with burglary if he or she admits to entering your library with the intent to steal something. Most crooks will not admit this to the police or prosecutors, saying they just got the impulse to steal something as they were walking around. Some states have a felony charge called "petty theft with a prior," meaning the person has already been convicted of prior petty theft cases and now every subsequent arrest can be charged as a burglary because he or she has demonstrated a pattern of multiple thefts. Shoplifters who steal from retail stores—and people who steal multiple times from the library—can be charged under this felony section if they have already been convicted of other thefts.

Our first best defense against people who try to steal things at the library is awareness. We have to be vigilant in our constant awareness to look for people who are engaging in "casing" behaviors, meaning they are looking for things to steal. This means they actually stare at, walk past several times, or keep looking at what they want to steal. This is how we can stop them, in that time between the urge to do it and doing it. We can interrupt their script, which operates the movie that is playing in their heads as they contemplate their theft behavior. "Hi, sir! I see you're looking at our game consoles. What types of games are you interested in playing? We have a great collection here." This is often more than enough to knock this person off the path from ideas to actions.

Another example: You see a patron slip a handful of DVDs into her backpack and start to head out the door. "Hi, ma'am! I can help you out at the desk over here if you're ready to check out your DVDs." If the person says, "I don't have any DVDs," you could say, "Oh, my mistake. I thought you had some in your backpack that you were just holding until you were ready to check them out. If you don't want to check them out, I can reshelve them for you."

The key to these approaches is to go with the flow, not cause a confrontation, and give the patron a face-saving way out. "Oh," she says, "I must have forgotten about these" as she hands the DVDs over to you. If the person tries to make a scene and say, "Are you accusing me of stealing!?," you can call over a colleague, the person in charge (PIC), or a supervisor, and say, "Of course not! I know you'd never do that. I just wanted to help you by holding on to our material until you're finally ready to check out." At that point, the patron has to either cough up the about-to-be-stolen DVDs and act like she didn't want them anyway, or quickly leave the premises, with or without them.

At no point should you ever chase anyone who has stolen any item from you, the library, or another patron. There are plenty of stories of security guards and even cops getting assaulted, stabbed, or shot by people they were trying to detain for shoplifting. None of these are in your job description.

Our second defense against people who steal from us is the use of consequences. Those of you with children and/or pets already know: no consequences for the behavior, then the behavior will continue. If people can steal successfully from us at the library, word will get around the streets that it's okay to do so, no harm, no foul. This is not the message we want to encourage.

Besides asking the person to return the materials they have hidden, no further questions or actions are necessary; we can also ban people who we know have stolen from us. The third choice is to make a citizen's arrest. For a petty theft not committed in front of a police officer, the library employee or patron who witnessed the theft will have to make a citizen's arrest in front of the police. (This scenario suggests the thief has not run out of the building, was detained by a uniformed library security officer, or is still arguing about it when the police arrive.)

Making a citizen's arrest sounds a lot more dramatic than it is—mostly because of how it is portrayed on TV, as either a comedy bit or as part of a police drama. It's a simple process: You say to the police officer, "I saw this person take my cell phone from my desk, place it in his pocket, and walk out of the building. I'd like to make a citizen's arrest for the theft." The officer will say, "Please sign this report form here, that says you are making a citizen's arrest, under penalty of perjury, and that you will agree to appear in court, if it goes that far, to testify to what you saw." You sign the form, and the officer will either cite and release the person with a theft charge, or arrest him or her and take the person to jail for petty theft.

Now if your smartphone is worth $800, you won't need to make a citizen's arrest because the officer can arrest the person without you for grand theft, a felony.

If you have to be a part of a citizen's arrest or a police report, ask the officer to use your work contact information, not your home contact information. The accused thief or his or her criminal defense attorney may get a copy of the arrest report, so there's no need to have your personal information on it.

Many people—including staffers at the library—would really "rather not get involved" in these types of stressful events, and that's perfectly understandable. But in petty theft cases, where a library employee or a patron witnessed a petty theft and chooses not to press the charges by making a citizen's arrest, there is not much the police can do. They can run the person for outstanding warrants, check them for being under the influence of drugs, and release the person with a stern warning not to steal at the library again.

Tell all patrons you cannot be everywhere and see everything, so they need to take good care of their personal belongings. Remind them not to wander off and leave a $1,200 cell phone sitting on the table.

Have the Courage—spelled with a capital C—to do the right thing on your behalf and send the message that it's not okay to steal from the library.

NOTES

1. Amy Sutherland, *What Shamu Taught Me about Life, Love, and Marriage: Lessons for People from Animals and Their Trainers* (New York: Random House, 2008), p. 85.
2. Kendra Cherry, "How Extinction Is Defined in Psychology," Verywell Mind, June 27, 2021, https://www.verywellmind.com/what-is-extinction-2795176.
3. Sutherland, *What Shamu Taught Me about Life, Love, and Marriage*, p. 45.
4. Barry Trott, interview with the author by telephone, June 30, 2022.
5. Jim Wining, personal interview with the author, February 22, 2022, Springfield, Missouri.

7

Working Safely in a Rural Location

THE ONE-EMPLOYEE OR MICRO-STAFF LIBRARY

The need to stay safe when help is far is a challenge most library employees don't have to face. If you're reading this book, chances are better than average that you work in a fairly large library facility, with plenty of coworkers, a director, a few department heads, some managers, and several supervisors or PICs (persons in charge). In short, there is probably more than one room for your library, there is a staff-only area that can be locked (or is accessible only by a key card) and is away from the prying eyes of the public and would-be trespassers, and you can get some peace, privacy, and feel mostly fully safe where you work. You probably have access to at least one secure, lockable "safe room," where you can shelter in place in the rare event of an armed attacker. This could be a staff restroom, staff break room, training room, storage or utility room, or other location off the main library floor and in a staff-only area that is behind another set of one or more locked doors or barricaded hallways. Or maybe not . . .

You may work at a small library, with only yourself and a few colleagues, or at what I would define as a micro-staff library (you and a coworker), or a one-person/one-room library, where you are the only person there, in charge of all you survey and all who enter. To complicate the security side a bit more, you might work in a small, micro, or one-person library and the closest law enforcement response is two hours away. Consider that the national average in the United States, from the time a 9-1-1 call gets placed and the police arrive, is around 10 minutes, depending on geography, traffic, weather, and staffing. So if we split the difference and say a cop is usually 10 minutes away from your location in an emergency, you can guess that two hours (or even 20 minutes) doesn't compare.

Working alone in a one- or two-room library, or working with just another colleague in a rural location, is a challenge at a lot of levels: boredom, loneliness, "Groundhog Day Again and Again" (same patrons, same small facility, not much excitement or variation to your workday).

From my perspective, it's safety and security first and optimal working conditions second, since you can only make your work satisfying if you feel safe while doing it. As such, the security-first mind-set you need in a single-person or small library is different than in a larger facility with lots of staffers because your resources are limited, help is far from you, and you probably have to deal with a lot of the same patron behavioral issues as if you worked in a larger library in a larger town. You may have just as many problems with your "Frequent Flier" patrons as a bigger library because you may be the only public building in your community where they feel comfortable going, day after day. You may know a lot of these patrons and their families, (and interesting behavioral histories in rich detail), which makes interacting with them all the more difficult than if you didn't know about them or their backgrounds. Certain small-town patrons may feel even more entitled to share their day and views on life with you, which perhaps can lead to rude comments, prying questions, other verbal or physical intrusions, or personal boundary issues into your physical space.

Local elected or appointed officials or even local law enforcement may not consider your workplace safety concerns—unless something serious happens—and they may hold the belief that "he or she is harmless or a little eccentric or just wants attention" when you describe certain difficult encounters with the local population who visit your library. This may certainly be true from their view, since they have had minimal or controlled dealings with them, none of which is the same as the library space and how the patrons see you in it. We shall discuss how to acquaint politicians with the realities of your library security needs in a moment. Just know that if you work alone or with only one or two colleagues (who may even be part-timers), I am watching out for you.

One of my colleagues described a process where you might need acting skills when working alone with patrons with eccentric habits, questionable sobriety, or uneven mental health. He referred to it as "street theater," meaning sometimes, when you are working alone and it's just you and him, or you and her, or you and them in your small library room, you may have to act more assertive than you actually feel. You may have to act as if you aren't uncomfortable when you really are. You may have to take charge when you feel like leaving the building or leave the building if the situation devolves into dangerousness. In other words, you'll need to fake it until you can make it, or "act as if" until the situation changes for the better (they wander out) or help arrives (to change the ratio of confrontation). Think creatively and become the director of your own "street theater."

MAKING YOUR LIBRARY SECURITY CASE WITH APPOINTED OR ELECTED OFFICIALS

When it comes to security in their respective workplaces, most people (who aren't me) tend to see the ocean through the diameter of their own small drinking straw. This means if a significant security threat or a near or an actual dangerous event hasn't ever happened to them or not for a long time, they discount the possibility that it could happen at all. This is especially true when you try to speak to your boss (who may work at a larger library or far from yours) or a library board about current, past, or potential patron behavioral issues—you may get your concerns ignored, minimized, or rationalized.

In every governmental organization, there are what we can call "safety and security stakeholders," who have the job duties, job description, and ethical imperative to protect the employees and the citizens of their towns. The larger the municipality, the more of these people there are because, in smaller towns, these government leaders will often have to fill several roles simultaneously. We can list the usual collection of "safety and security stakeholders" as the police chief, or sheriff, the fire chief, the state police commander for the area, the town manager, the city manager, the chief administrative officer, the personnel director, the facilities director, and/or public works director, the risk manager or safety officer (if those roles exist), the IT director, and the town, city, or district attorney.

There are others depending on how your municipality is arranged, but this list covers most of the roles that have built into them a requirement to protect people and property. With the proper education, motivation, and explanations from you, these officials can help you get the security improvements you seek, especially if you're the library director for your town. If you aren't the library director, I'm not suggesting you leap over the chain of command and go over your boss's head, only that you recognize the value of personal conversations with these stakeholders if your boss cannot or will not help you.

When speaking with them, don't take "It's not in the budget for this year" or "That's just how it is" or "That's how it has always been" as answers for your requests for policy changes, new or updated security equipment, or responses to an incident. I'm not saying you should argue so much that you put your job at risk, only that you may need to bring assertiveness and evidence to this important discussion. Use any Security Incident Reports for the past year to build your case for policy changes and security improvements. Be ready to give your elected officials and library leaders (if you aren't one) solutions instead of just complaints. This doesn't mean you'll want to bring a laundry list of dozens of requests. Keep your list of ideas short, useful, and budget-conscious, at least for now. You already know security in libraries is a work in progress, and we are most often driven by events. Make your case with factual incidents, not emotional anecdotes.

One place to build your security case in a rural library setting is by taking ideas from other libraries and librarians with similar issues, in similarly sized communities, who have improved their security posture in creative or cost-effective ways. Talk with your colleagues and see how they have overcome the various bureaucratic hurdles that come with making security improvements. Research recent national workplace violence, school violence, and workplace domestic violence cases to emphasize the continuous problems in these areas. Collect cases of crimes of violence that have happened in libraries, to patrons or employees, to support your need for changes.

Discuss your concerns with elected and appointed stakeholders about employee safety, the need to minimize any workers' compensation injuries, litigation claims, insurance policy and renewal costs, employee retention and morale issues, and increased liability for staff and patrons. Keep the focus on both the people side of the library business and the business side of the library business. You might want to carefully mention the phrase "bad optics" to government leaders, as it relates to negative public opinions and negative mainstream or social media stories about the need for better library employee safety and security.

Be willing to make your case to a variety of audiences beyond the usual government resources: library boards, Friends of the Library, local civic and community groups (e.g., Lions, Elks, Optimists, Kiwanis, or VFW), and local businesses that might want to donate security equipment to their local library.

In the end, let the electeds and appointeds be the heroes in the local media; just have them help you get what you need to feel safer at your workspace.

WORKING ALONE

What follows are some ideas for protecting yourself when working alone in a small library, especially if it's in a rural community. (In the next section, I'll present some suggestions for working with your colleagues in a small library environment; both sets of tips apply. Take what you need to feel more secure in both environments.) More than a few of these ideas fall into a category I use often in security discussions, known as "outside-the-box" thinking. In other words, they may sound a little impractical, not feasible, or even odd. I created them knowing that sometimes you have to take complete charge of your own safety, and you can feel better knowing that these ideas work, if you give them a chance or can get permission to use them. Hear me out and let's jump right in.

CREATE A TWICE-DAILY CHECK-IN CALL PROTOCOL WITH ANOTHER LIBRARY

In my Perfect Library World, staffers or supervisors from a larger library near you would call and speak to you, at least twice per day, and not necessarily just at the start of your shift or at the end of it. The purpose of these check-ins, of course, is to make certain you are breathing and vertical. You might also consider developing a code word, or better yet, a coded phrase, that would alert them to call 9-1-1 on your behalf if you say it, because that means you're dealing with a dangerous patron or are under duress. "I can't find the Purple File" could be a useful sentence to tell the staffer on the other end you need emergency help.

INSTALL A CAMERA SYSTEM THAT CAN BE MONITORED OFFSITE

If the two-phone-calls-a-day approach is part one of staying safe in a rural library environment, then part two is to have a camera system set up in your facility (at your main working desk or providing a view of where you're most likely to be all day) that can be monitored by other library supervisors or staffers at their location. Thanks to the internet, these remote view setups (which started back in the "nanny cam" days) make it easy to show your work area remotely. There's no need for an audio hookup; just have them pay attention to your camera view on an irregular basis to see if you look like you might need emergency help. Signs about cameras being on the premises and "No Firearms Allowed" don't stop crime, but they do remind some people that we do take security seriously. You can post interior and exterior signs about being recorded that have a bit of a light touch: "Wave to the Camera!" Try to avoid signs that sound stupidly bureaucratic, like "Premises under Video Surveillance." If there are other predominant languages, besides English, which are used in your area, consider posting bilingual signs too.

ASK THE SURROUNDING BUSINESSES TO CHECK ON YOU

If your rural library is located in a strip mall or along a road where there are other businesses, introduce yourself and ask if the owners, supervisors, or employees can just do an occasional drive-by wave at you as they go about their days. One rural library I recall was near the local volunteer fire department, and so the firefighters on their shifts would check on the library staffer from time to time. You could be situated near the state police barracks, which may have only a few troopers working in it, and they could provide a similar courtesy for you and your building.

HIRE A PART-TIME SECURITY PATROL

Many communities have a few local security guard companies that service construction sites, strip malls, apartment complexes, and other clients where they either get out and do a quick walk-through or just drive by. For not much money each month, you can put your library facility on their daily spot-check list and pay them to come by once, twice, or six times per day, depending on their rates. I have done this on a similar basis when it comes to my small-business clients that take in a lot of cash, by hiring an armored car service that is already working in their area. It's cheap insurance and extra peace of mind.

INSTALL A PANIC ALARM THAT RINGS TO A LOCAL OR LIVE-ANSWER MONITORING ALARM COMPANY

Like the camera system improvements we have seen over the years, alarm systems, including personal panic alarms worn on the body, have become common and much less expensive to install and monitor. Panic alarms for libraries can be installed under the main Circulation or Information desks and even in employees-only work areas. Personal panic alarms are small, light, and unobtrusive. Pressing the panic alarm button should trigger a response by an alarm company to call and check on you and dispatch the police/sheriff if they cannot reach you. These aren't bullet-proof shields, only ways of enhancing your security posture when working alone.

TALK TO YOUR "PHANTOM COWORKER" WHEN ENCOUNTERING A PATRON WHO MAKES YOU FEEL UNCOMFORTABLE

Okay, I'll admit this sounds and looks goofy on its face, but I have done it many times and I know it works. I used to teach robbery prevention for a major gasoline/convenience store chain in California. I would tell the clerks working alone to call out to a "coworker" who is not actually there, whenever they felt uncomfortable with someone in their stores. Shouting, "Keep stocking the backroom, Larry! I'll take care of this gentleman who just walked in" is a phrase they used and you can use to suggest to a possible bad guy that you are not alone. The idea of the "phantom colleague" is to at least insert doubt in the minds of potentially scary people that there may be a (male) witness in the back. It's all about deterrence.

GET PERMISSION TO HAVE OC PEPPER SPRAY AT YOUR LIBRARY

OC stands for *Oleoresin Capsicum* (Latin for "My eyeballs are on fire!"), and in days of old, people used to call it "mace," which is actually something completely different. I have been a training instructor for OC pepper spray for many years, and I have been doused so many times, I put the stuff on my eggs in the morning. Seriously, it works on bad people and mean dogs. It stings and it burns the person or beast who gets a face full, but the damage is not permanent, and it buys you time and distance to get away safely and call the police. There are two usual problems when it comes to bringing OC to the library environment: many administrators don't understand it and therefore ban it by policy, and most people who do get permission to carry it don't have it near their hands when they really need it. If you carry a purse or a backpack, having your can of OC pepper spray at the bottom is not useful. It's also of little value locked in your desk drawer, in the center console or glove compartment in your car, or at home.

Let's address the first issue: getting permission to carry OC. If you're an employee and want to have OC at the library, reassure your boss you'll take full responsibility for its safe storage (which, ideally, is concealed on your actual person) and its reasonable use as a defensive tool (to protect me from an assault; it's not reasonable to call it an "offensive weapon" because the vast majority of people who ever have to use it are protecting themselves, not harming others.)

For the second issue, OC comes in small canisters, with a safety top to prevent accidental spraying, and can be kept in your pocket. Buy the can with the highest concentration percentage of OC you can find—not .004 percent but more like 1 percent. This sounds sadistically masochistic (or masochistically sadistic), but you should test OC on your own face. Spray a small dab on your finger and wipe it just under (not in) your eye. It will burn and cause tearing, but guess what? It's not fatal, and you can still back away or run away from your attacker, or leave the building and get police help, even with some splashed on you. That is the point of the exercise—to know how it works on your face and that you can still function. (Wash your face carefully with a diluted mixture of water and baby shampoo.) The other value to testing it on yourself is that you will know what it feels like and your attacker may not. Most crooks have never been paper sprayed, and that's why it works so well on them—surprise, burning, blinding pain. You will be ahead of them if you've already tested it.

GET PERMISSION TO BRING YOUR DOG TO WORK

Like OC pepper spray, unless you're in charge of your single-employee library, you'll probably have to get permission to bring your dog to work. This is a touchy area, to be sure. No library needs to have a Schutzhund-trained police dog lounging around on the carpet in the stacks. But if you have a well-behaved medium- to large-sized dog who could serve as a useful deterrent to anyone who wants to harm you, might you be able to bring your dog to work with you? (I have Pugs and Chihuahuas, which are fun but have no deterrent value, unless you count day-long napping as a security deterrent.)

HAVE AN ESCAPE PLAN

Know how and when to get out of your building. This is another area where I can get disagreements from library staffers. "I can't just leave the building unoccupied! I have to stay there, no matter what is going on." I would suggest this is both admirable and wrong. If the library building was on fire, you would not hesitate to abandon ship. If you are being threatened by someone while you work alone and you can leave the building safely, creatively, or even secretly, do so. Get into your car (which needs to be parked as close to the main entrance/exit or rear doors as possible) and drive away, calling for help on your cell phone as you do.

HIDE YOUR VALUABLES IN A SAFE PLACE IN THE BUILDING

Create a "robbery pack" (fake keys, wallet, small amount of cash, purse, old cell phone), which, again, is another tool I taught the gas station clerks during my past trainings. Working alone in a library, you could be susceptible to an attack or a robbery. The robber wants what he or she can grab from you, off you, or near you, so don't have any of your personal belongings on you, except your cell phone. Store your purse, backpack, wallet, cash, personal car/house keys in a lockable file cabinet in your office. If you are confronted for your valuables, give the robber a fake set of keys, an old cell phone, a purse, a wallet with a few dollars in it, and let this person run out. You don't want them stealing your car, armed with your driver's license and your address, driving to your home, and using your garage door opener or your keys to get inside and stealing everything from there, too.

Don't fight for your valuables; give them a fake set instead.

CREATE THE "SAFEST SAFE ROOM"

Find a room where you can lock or barricade the door and shelter in place until law enforcement arrives. In my Perfect Library World, this room would be sturdy, lockable, and have a good lock and metal frame that can't be kicked open. Maybe there is no such place in your library other than one of your restrooms. So be it.

RAMP UP YOUR ASSERTIVENESS AS YOU IMPLEMENT YOUR CODE OF CONDUCT FIRMLY, FAIRLY, CONSISTENTLY, AND REASONABLY

Working alone all day takes courage, even when things feel completely safe. Working alone when you feel threatened is harrowing. You may need to act more assertively than usual when you're asking a problematic patron to leave.

TALK YOUR WAY OUT OF CONFRONTATIONS AND/OR "LEAVE CREATIVELY" BY EASING YOUR WAY OUT OF THE BUILDING

There is a value, in my experience, when dealing with potentially threatening people, to finding a way out of the room and even out of the building.

MAKE BOLD SAFETY DECISIONS WHEN YOU FEEL YOU MUST

As I have said many times in my library security trainings and in this book, you need to follow the "Lifeguard Model" when it comes to personal safety. Take care of yourself first (a lifeguard can't drown at the beach), take care of your coworkers second (a lifeguard saves his or her colleagues), and take care of the patrons third (you are no good to others if you're not first safe yourself). Nowhere in your job description does it say you need to do anything heroic outside of those three responses.

WORKING WITH ONE OR MORE COLLEAGUES

With the following suggestions, you have the luxury of working with at least one to two coworkers in your facility. You may have a bigger building than just a one-room library, you may have more than one entrance/exit door, and your "safe room/shelter in place room" options are perhaps greater. Having a coworker to watch your interactions with typically challenging patrons is always useful, but keep in mind that most of the safety and security options listed for solo work will be as effective with a colleague. Some tools work best with other like-minded coworkers who are also focused on having a safe and peaceful workday for all of you.

DEVELOP CODE WORDS AND HAND SIGNALS

In my training classes, I typically suggest you and your colleagues spend a few moments defining (and committing to memory) a set of code words and hand signals for security issues. I use two main hand signals when I want the attention of a coworker to come help me, either at my side or near enough to see/hear what is happening but not too close to me: index finger pointed at your colleague and then joining at your feet. This means, "Come join me." Second approach: index finger pointed at your colleague, followed by a palm-up (fingers pointed up gesture), which means, "Come close and watch from a bit of a distance." Use the first one when you want collaboration in front of the challenging patron. Use the second one when you want observation, so your colleague can see what he or she is saying or doing, but by staying a bit back, it doesn't feel like we are crowding the patron.

Staffers should develop two sets of verbal code words. One should mean: "Go to a safe place and call the police/sheriff." The other should mean, "Leave the building now!" As two examples, when I lived and worked in California we used phrases like, "Go get Mr. Arnold" (as in former governor and movie actor Arnold Schwarzenegger) to send an employee to call 9-1-1 in a safe location. You can also use the uniform color of the local police or sheriff's agency, as in, "Please call Mrs. Green" (sheriff's deputies in many of California's fifty-eight counties wear dark green pants). The phrase to evacuate can be something like, "You're needed in the conference room." (Most small or rural libraries don't have a conference room; this means leave the building immediately.) Pick any phrases that work best for you and your colleagues. They need to be short, catchy, and memorable.

TALK WITH EACH OTHER ABOUT HOW TO HANDLE YOUR PROBLEMATIC "FREQUENT FLIERS," USING A CONSISTENT APPROACH

Most small libraries get the same people coming in, day after week after year. You may be a better fit for some patrons, and your colleague may be a better fit for others. Debrief if you have a difficult encounter and talk about what worked and what potential "hot buttons" you both might want to avoid with the patron for the next time. Collaborate and come up with useful "talking points" for the patrons you see most often.

DISCUSS WHEN A PERMANENT BAN OR CIVIL ORDER MAY BE NECESSARY

Sometimes all you can do is all you can do, and despite your best efforts at communication, de-escalation, patience, and negotiated accommodations ("I'll agree to do this for you if you will agree to do that for me"), it's not enough and the patron needs more significant boundaries. If you have collected a pile of Security Incident Reports (SIRs) and there is no change or the patron's problem behaviors are in fact escalating, it may be time to get a restraining order. These documents are by no means a bulletproof shield and they don't really work if the restrained person is not a rule follower, but they have value for the staff and for law enforcement, especially when they are enforced correctly and each time they are violated by the patron. Your city attorney, town attorney, or district or prosecuting attorney can review the patron's case file and help you decide if a Temporary Restraining Order (TRO) will help.

CREATE BETTER SIGHT LINES, ELIMINATE BLIND SPOTS, AND DO YOUR WALKAROUNDS

This is your work location, so set it up to accommodate your needs, not just for the convenience of the patrons. If you can't see around certain blind corners, redesign the shelving or display areas. If you have camera views that go nowhere, don't display well in low light, or need repair, get that work ordered. Your working space should feel open, so you can sit or stand at various parts of the library building and see as much as you need to see. Don't trade good visual sightlines for the aesthetics of the furniture. Move, reposition, or eliminate what is in your way.

CREATE AN "ICE BOX" FOR ALL EMPLOYEES (IN CASE OF EMERGENCY)

This should be an actual accessible plastic box that contains a first aid kit (including enough tourniquets), a laminated and updated list of callback/callout numbers for emergency officials or senior library leaders, an extra set of hard keys and key cards or key fobs (to give to first responders, if necessary).

PERSONAL SAFETY

Who else can help you in an emergency? Who is in your community? State police? Local fire department? Junior college police? University police? K-12 school police? Railroad police?

KNOW THE OPEN-CARRY AND CONCEALED-CARRY FIREARMS LAWS FOR YOUR STATE

These vary by state and even by county and city ordinance. Some local municipalities have strict rules about carrying firearms—exposed or concealed, even with a permit—into municipal buildings, libraries included. Other agencies have not weighed in on the issue and leave it up to the local library. You may or may not have the right to deny patrons access to your building with an openly displayed firearm or a concealed firearm. These laws can change with every election cycle. Get a legal update to know for certain.

USE THE DURESS ALARM FUNCTION ON THE BUILDING'S BURGLAR ALARM

If you cannot get a personal panic alarm and you have a monitored perimeter burglar alarm installed at your facility (which is a useful and worthwhile investment), see if the system includes a "duress button" feature. This is useful for those times when you may be working alone or with a colleague and the library is closed. Should someone try to break in when you are inside, the alarm will ring. This feature won't work if your alarm system is only activated by motion detectors mounted on the ceiling.

INSTALL A DESK-MOUNTED FRONT DOOR LOCK

Get a desk-mounted front door lock installed that you can operate from a desk. Consider how many doctors' offices work, where the receptionist buzzes you into the treatment area from the desk, without having to get up to open the door. Many professional offices are designed this way, with security at the reception or administration desk and a button that the employee can press to allow access by job applicants, visitors, vendors, and customers. You should have the same ability to lock or unlock your door from your desk. This is most useful for those patrons who make serious violence threats to return—for example, "I'm going to my car, and you'll be sorry when I get back!" You can lock the door and call 9-1-1 without having to go to the door to do it.

INSIST ON A REAR EXIT DOOR

If you work in a one-room library, where the main entry/exit door is in the front and could be blocked by an angry patron, you need an alternative way out. Have your facilities / maintenance / public works colleagues cut a new door behind you or in a back hallway, that you can use to escape. Unless your library is a protected historic facility that cannot be changed, you should be able to get this done. Get some support from the local fire marshal to help your case for this.

Working Safely in a Rural Location

ENCOURAGE REGULAR VISITS BY YOUR FAMILY, FRIENDS, AND TRUSTED PATRONS

Any extra eyes and ears upon you and your facility can be a good thing. Similarly, connect with nearby businesses, supportive neighbors, K–12 school, trade school, or college employees who might be willing to check on you.

CONSIDER OFFERING MORE COMMUNITY OR GROUP PROGRAMS

Let community service groups (e.g., Kiwanis, Optimists, Soroptimists, Lions) use your space for their monthly meetings.

PRACTICE SITUATIONAL AWARENESS

Have just as much situational awareness during daylight hours as you would during nighttime hours. We tend to be much more vigilant at night because that's when we think most crimes occur. Banks get robbed in the daytime, and lots of other bad things happen when the sun is high. Pay constant attention to your personal safety no matter the time of day.

PROTECT YOURSELF WITH "SECRET SERVICE HANDS"

Put your hands into a prayer position, about even with the top of your belly button, with your wrists touching your stomach. This pyramid pose is one I use in those rare situations where I feel I may have to defend myself. With my hands in this posture, I can push away someone who tries to touch me or violate my space, or I can block someone coming into my space. It's called "Secret Service hands" because that's how their agents stand. (You'll find plenty of images online of them protecting various presidents that will prove my point.)

It's a nonconfrontational posture, which serves three self-defense-related purposes: it gives you something useful to do with your hands in a stressful discussion with a problematic person, it's a common gesture that people make when they feel confident (watch talk shows and see how often it is used by experts who feel comfortable with their opinions), and it can serve as an attention-getting gesture for one of your coworkers to come over and help you. Get used to using it.

WATCH THE TWO RUN-HIDE-FIGHT VIDEOS AT LEAST ONCE PER YEAR

As I will suggest in the next chapter on responding to the rare possibility of an armed attacker in your library, there are lots of ways to educate yourself and your coworkers on the now-standard "Run-Hide-Fight" suggested approach to an active shooter in your library. There are videos on YouTube, some good, others awful, and a few excellent.

One video is the standard government response to this national problem, a training segment created by the Department of Homeland Security (DHS) and the City of Houston, Texas. I like the video but I don't love it. It can be a bit jarring, even for a serious topic like a mass shooter. Perhaps I feel that way because I have shown it hundreds of times and I see some library employees cringe through certain parts.

Given my preference, I really like a similar Run-Hide-Fight video created by the California State University system. It covers the same issues as the DHS version, but with a bit more empathy for the viewers, and it is more empowering as opposed to overpowering.

8

Armed Attacker in the Library

RARE, CATASTROPHIC, AND SURVIVABLE

> If you're a lifeguard at the beach, the first person you need to save in any water emergency is yourself. You are no good to the person you're trying to save if you drown. Take care of yourself first; take care of everyone else second.
>
> —Lifeguard's Credo

My version of this credo for library folks is similar. When it comes to keeping yourself safe at the library, the order is just like it would be at the beach or a deep swimming pool: "Take care of yourself first. Take care of your coworkers second. Take care of the patron third."

"But Dr. Steve, what if there is an active-shooter event in our library? What about the patrons who can't move as quickly to evacuate or shelter in place, like our seniors or little kids?"

I hear you. "Take care of yourself first. Take care of your coworkers second. Take care of the patron third." You cannot help others in an armed attacker situation if you're not alive or safe first.

The creation of this chapter sits in the shadow of two horrific events in the long and tragic collection of workplace and school shootings in the United States: the Buffalo, New York, grocery store shooting on May 14, 2022, that claimed ten lives and the Uvalde, Texas, school shooting that left nineteen children and two adults dead on May 24, 2022. These incidents continue, despite the best efforts of people like me, who work in threat assessment and threat management[1]; the local police, who may have to respond to these attacks with limited information and not a lot of tactical training; and the survivors, who have to deal with life after the deaths of those around them—loved ones, strangers, children, students, shoppers, adults, and employees.

Once again we are faced with a national tragedy that affects the safety and enhances the fears of everyone, with another mass shooting, this time at a Texas elementary school. It's just too hard to deal with, especially coming just after another mass shooting at a Buffalo, New York, grocery store. There is no end in sight to these events, regardless of what our legislators do at the national and state levels. The police response is one solution, but as we have seen in Texas, it's not a perfect solution.

After thirty years as a security consultant in these areas, I feel as you probably do: defeated, angry, pessimistic, sad for the families of the lost, furious at the perpetrators, angry at the lack of solutions, and anxious about the death toll and location of the next event. Therefore, when it comes to our safety and security at public-access buildings, like our schools, stores, and libraries, it is up to the employees and their leaders to respond, improvise, adapt, and do all they can to protect themselves and the people inside.

The design parallels between the inside of a public library and the inside of a K-12 public school are obvious once we compare them: open seating areas; lots of tables, desks, and chairs; multiple entrances and exits; hallways; stairwells and staircases; restrooms; staff-only areas; blind spots and poorly lit areas; bookshelves and books; storage areas; IT server rooms; and utility rooms. There are specific lessons to be learned, by library leaders and staffers, from the Uvalde school tragedy, which they can directly apply to help deny, deter, delay, and stop an armed attacker during the rare possibility of an active-shooter event. There are important steps to take before an attack (look for signs of information leakage by a potential attacker; protect the facility with better access control); during an attack (Run-Hide-Fight); and after an attack (initiate traumatic stress debriefings).

Let's look at all three of these areas, and give an in-depth review of what takes place during the structured debriefing process following a highly traumatic event. The more you know about that process, the better you can help yourself and your colleagues heal if it ever happens at your facility.

Active shooters and armed attackers coming into a workplace, K-12 school, library, college or university, theater, or mall to kill people is devastating, horrific, chaotic, and fortunately, rarer than the media would like you to believe. There have certainly been more incidents in the last ten years, but the chances of you being injured or killed by a person with a gun are highly unlikely, especially if you don't work in a retail environment, in a health care setting, or at night, all of which tend to have higher risks of violence. (Men commit the majority of these crimes; some women have been perpetrators as well. It's important not to generalize when it comes to these attackers or their motives, but for this subject, we will most often use the pronoun "he.")

KEY THEMES OF LIBRARY WORKPLACE VIOLENCE PREVENTION

These are core ideas to consider as we view recent attacks with an eye toward better protecting our staff, patrons, and facilities. There are no guarantees of safety and nothing is shooter-proof, but these concepts might make a life-or-death difference if you can consider them and/or put them in place at your library.

These concepts make sense, based on the decades of research and review of the multitude of school and workplace violence incidents; mass attacks at concerts, malls, movie theaters, and hospitals; and domestic violence cases, where employees are targeted by their former partners. Each of these eleven builds on the others, and library employees are connected to and should be aware of them all.

FAIR, ETHICAL, EMPATHIC, AND CONSISTENT TREATMENT OF ALL PATRONS AND STAFF

How we treat patrons and how we treat each other, as human beings all just trying to get by in the world, makes a huge difference in violence prevention. Why? Not only because it's the ethical, empathic, right thing to do, but mostly because most workplace and school violence incidents are driven by the perpetrator's desire for revenge. How we treat patrons in the service part of library interactions, and how we treat employees in the human resources interactions, makes a huge difference in calming this desire for revenge, to pay someone back for being mistreated.

RAPPORT BUILDING, KINDNESS, EMPATHY, PATIENCE, AND ENHANCED LISTENING SKILLS MAKE A DIFFERENCE

How we treat patrons and employees, especially during their most stressful moments, goes a long way toward either enhancing or decreasing their desire to come back to do harm by using revenge as their motivation. Fair, empathic, and patient treatment of patrons (even when they give none of these things back to us) and legal, empathic, and humane HR policies and practices for employees facing discipline or termination can and has been shown to prevent violence.

LISTEN FOR PRE-ATTACK LEAKAGE: VERBAL, SOCIAL, ELECTRONIC

We have realized that most perpetrators leak what they are going to do—verbally, on paper, electronically, or through social media. As the US Secret Service and the FBI have taught me for so many years, they don't leak to their desired targets; they tell other people around those targets. This is known as "third-party leakage," where the potential attacker threatens to do harm via someone near the target, not their actual intended target. The reasons for this are many, but we need to tell our safety and security stakeholders when we hear leaked threats. What you hear in passing may be enough to stop a frustrated patron from acting out, when you have the courage to tell the safety and security stakeholders in your library (e.g., the director, HR, department heads, managers, supervisors, security managers, risk managers, IT and facilities managers, the agency attorney).

USE ACCESS CONTROL AND SECURITY DEVICES ALL DAY, EVERY DAY

Keep the staff on the staff side and the patrons on the patron side.

Access control and locked doors make a difference. Key cards and panic alarms matter, so use them. Keep staff-only entrance doors locked at all times. Yes, it's a hassle to fish out a door key or (better yet) a key card, but we should never trade security for convenience. Keep all non-employees on the other side of our locked doors.

FOLLOW THE RUN-HIDE-FIGHT PROTOCOL

Schedule an annual (empowering, not frightening) Run-Hide drill.

We react under stress to what we have been trained to do. Without proper training, we make the wrong moves and can make a bad situation worse. There is no need to frighten library staff with SWAT team scenarios or fake guns. Just practice a calm, controlled Run-Hide drill once per year, talk about it before and after as a staff, watch the Run-Hide-Fight videos I have suggested, and get back to work.

TOURNIQUETS, AUTOMATED EXTERNAL DEFIBRILLATOR (AED) MACHINES, CPR TRAINING, AND FULLY STOCKED FIRST AID KITS MATTER

For maximum effectiveness, we should stock our library first aid kits with enough tourniquets and clotting bandages for several dozen people. Mass injury events will need more than the usual one or two of everything found in most first aid kits. Get trained in AED use, basic CPR, and "stop the bleed" tourniquet use (www.stopthebleed.org/).

SOCIAL MEDIA POSTINGS AND MESSAGES ABOUT OUR LIBRARIES OR OUR EMPLOYEES NEED TO BE ANALYZED

Some school districts, private-sector businesses, and public-sector agencies subscribe to social media monitoring services, which can tell them immediately if their organization is named on the usual social media sites in connection to a threat. It's not a bad idea for the library to pay for similar oversight.

IT'S STILL THE "LONE WOLF MALES" WHO ARE COMMITTING THESE ATTACKS

It's possible more than one shooter is at one site, but not very likely. There have been only a handful of multiple-attacker events in the United States in the last thirty years: the Oklahoma City Federal Building bombing in 1995; the

Columbine High School attackers in 1999; the pair of Washington DC snipers in 2002; the Boston Marathon bombings in 2013; and the San Bernardino Inland Regional Center attack by husband and wife terrorists in 2015. Violence is usually committed by angry, depressed, despondent, desperate, vengeful males of all ages and races. Women have committed acts of violence at their work facilities and on college campuses but certainly not to the extent of men. Pay attention to those males who seem to display what we could call "entitled disgruntlement." They are angry at everybody and everything, all the time, and their pre-attack behaviors often draw our attention.

COVER AND CONCEALMENT MATTER

Cover is steel, stone, or heavy wood bullet-stoppers. Concealment is curtains, drapes, blinds, tinted glass, masonry walls, and wooden or aluminum doors. Get behind cover first; hide behind concealment if cover is not close or safely accessible.

DON'T SPEAK TO THE MEDIA UNLESS YOU ARE TRAINED AND DESIGNATED BY THE LIBRARY TO DO SO

As we have seen in the Uvalde, Texas, elementary school shooting, there is a lot of second-guessing going on in the media. Only give comments if you are the library's media representative. Refer all requests for comments to that person or the director.

ESTABLISH POST-TRAUMA COUNSELING EXPERTISE NOW

Get support for post-traumatic stress disorder (PTSD) now, from your Employee Assistance Program (EAP) provider, local mental health clinicians (with whom you should already be acquainted before a traumatic incident), and your local psychological association if you have one. These are career-ending, life-harming, mentally dangerous events. Every employee in the library who was exposed to or heard about a traumatic event has the right to ask for and get clinical care.

In my Perfect Library World, you would have already created a working relationship with local EAP professionals, local doctorates and doctors of psychology, trained in crisis response and trauma debriefing models.

Also useful are police or fire department chaplains, county social workers, Red Cross crisis managers, and crisis-trained community volunteers.

Help staff cope immediately when safe to do so. The counselors should provide symptom education, calm their fears, and prepare them for their first night. They will also triage the employees based on their trauma exposure and get hospital care for the most severely traumatized.

They should work with library leadership on the next day's steps and develop a primary, secondary, and tertiary staff help list.

THE RUN-HIDE-FIGHT MODEL (DEMYSTIFIED)

In order, the Run-Hide-Fight process means that if an armed attacker enters your library, your first best choice would be to *run*. Leave the building as safely and as quickly as possible, taking as many patrons and staff as you can, to avoid the shooter. This means leaving your work items and only taking what you can carry, quickly and safely, with you (purse, wallet, cell phone). If you're on the ground floor and you're trapped in your workspace, you may have to break a window and climb out. The key is to move out quickly and get away from the danger, taking as many coworkers or patrons with you. As you leave, if you encounter any first responders (police, firefighters, paramedics), be sure to give them your hard keys or electronic access key cards so they can move about the building safely and not get trapped in a locked hallway. We've seen too many examples of police officers and paramedics getting trapped in hallways where they don't have hard keys or key cards to get them into the interior of the building. Take this important step to give them your key card to speed up their tactical response.

If getting out is not possible or safe, for your second preferred choice, you'll need to find a place to *hide out*. This could be a break room, restroom, supervisor's office, storage room, file room, or even a closet. The key is to stay away from the shooter, lock or barricade the door as best as you can, stay out of the doorway (otherwise known as the "fatal funnel"), and wait for the arrival of the police. If you can safely call the police, using your cell phone, or better yet, a landline in the room, do so. Otherwise, turn off the lights, put as many heavy items as you can in front of the door, and stay quiet and as calm as you can, behind the relative safety of a locked or barricaded windowless room. We know these shooters don't shoot through a closed door to kill people or have ever impersonated the police from the other side of the door. The police response is forthcoming, with the national average within five to ten minutes. Every law enforcement agency in the United States knows this approach, and most of their members have been trained to use it as their response to an armed perpetrator.

Your third and final (and necessary choice) is to *fight back* against the attacker, using whatever objects (a pot of hot coffee or heavy books thrown at the attacker's face; chairs, desks, or tables carried by several people) or actual or improvised weapons (knives, OC pepper spray, a fire extinguisher) to stop the attacker if he makes entry into your safe room.

Some key points: if the room you are hiding in cannot be locked or it opens from the outside, try to use a belt or electrical cord to tie up the door-closing mechanism at the top (or tie two double doors together).

If you hear the fire alarm during a real active-shooter situation, and you do not see flames or smell smoke, stay put. We have seen some attackers pull the fire alarm to get people into their kill zones. Scared employees or supervisors have pulled the fire alarm in their buildings in the mistaken belief that this will either expedite the police response or warn people to get out of the building. Pulling the fire alarm in a non-fire situation only creates more noise and adds to the chaos. Stay in your safe room until you're notified by the police or other first responders that it's safe to evacuate.

If you choose to leave your building during a real active-shooter event, you may be able to drive or run to alternative evacuation locations located near your library, like a church, store, mall, open government office, fire, police, or sheriff's station. The key is to get away to wait in or near a safe location (you don't necessarily have to go inside one of these buildings), so you can connect with coworkers and wait out the event in safety.

To help you reinforce the critical Run-Hide-Fight concepts, watch one or both of two useful videos connected to the subject. The first is the *Run-Hide-Fight* video cocreated by the Department of Homeland Security (DHS) and the City of Houston, Texas. It's short and to the point. Here's a link to the City of Houston YouTube version: https://www.youtube.com/watch?v=5VcSwejU2D0.

The second video option provides an even more effective message. It was created by the California State University system, and it's an animated version of the Run-Hide-Fight approach. It may appeal to younger library employees and is perhaps more empowering and less frightening than the DHS version. Both are useful and bear watching, at least once per year for yourself and then again as part of a staff meeting conversation about how to respond to an active-shooter situation. Here's a link to the California State University YouTube version: https://www.youtube.com/watch?v=VUErkf3XEEs.

Use recent or previous workplace, school-based, health care, or library-related violence incidents as a teaching tool for your employees. You don't have to obsess over these events; use what happened as a way to stop the same thing from happening where you work.

Work with your safety and security stakeholders to create emergency phrases to be used over the facility's public address (PA) paging or notification systems. As an example, hospitals use color codes for various emergency events: Code Red (fire), Code Silver (person with a gun), and Code Orange (chemical spill or gas leak). This type of color code system may be useful in a building with a lot of public traffic, so employees can focus on taking the necessary evacuation or shelter-in-place steps without scaring the public.

Any paging message should focus on what the issue is (fire, gas leak, earthquake, weather event, active shooter), where it is happening (location, building, floor), and what to do next (evacuate, shelter in place, move to a certain location, or just flee, etc.). For events like real active shooters on the property, use the phrase "unusual incident" or "unusual event" to describe it, instead of saying "active shooter" over the PA. Train and remind all employees about your designated code words, since they won't work in an emergency if the employees won't remember them or don't know what to do.

Besides showing either or both Run-Hide-Fight videos, see if you can get senior management to agree to stage an annual "Fifteen-Minute Run-Hide Drill." This simply means that like staging a fire drill, an earthquake drill, or any other emergency drill, you set aside fifteen minutes, once per year, at some point in the workday to ask your employees to demonstrate the two steps to the three-step active-shooter response: *Leave* the building for fifteen minutes or *hide out* in some locked or barricaded part of the building for fifteen minutes (their choice). If you walk around during the drill and can't see them outside or in the rooms they have chosen to lock down, then they have done the drill successfully. That's it, and then they can go back to work. No need to demonstrate the third step, *fight*, unless it was an actual active-shooter emergency.

Sometimes senior management will balk at doing a Run-Hide drill because they think it's frivolous or a waste of time or, worse yet, that it will somehow scare the employees. As a director, manager, or supervisor, your defense should be that we don't need to set an actual fire in the building to help employees know what to do in a real fire emergency. We still practice fire drills annually even though we assume every employee will know what to do if the building caught on fire or they smelled smoke or a gas leak.

Under stress and especially under life-threatening stress, most people revert to how they have been trained, told, or taught. This includes airline pilots and air traffic controllers, police officers and firefighters, paramedics, nurses, and doctors, who get extensive live, hands-on, stress-inducing training at the earliest stages of their careers and throughout them. This is why the Run-Hide portion of the overall Run-Hide-Fight response is so important to practice at least once per year.

You may hear of an alternative Run-Hide-Fight model, which is mostly designed for K-12 schools. It's called ALICE, and it stands for Alert—Lockdown—Inform—Counter—Evacuate. This parallel alternative to the Run-Hide-Fight model was first developed by a police officer following the April 2000 Columbine High School shooting in Littleton, Colorado, which left thirteen killed by two students of the school. Both models work, in their respective workplace or school-based environments.

CHAPTER SUMMARY

- Watch (or rewatch) the Run-Hide-Fight video again, especially during an annual staff meeting.
- Consider showing it at home (make sure it is age appropriate).
- Remind all staff to trust their intuition, dial 9-1-1, and remember Run-Hide-Fight.
- Establish your clinical trauma response and prevention resources (EAP, local providers).
- Meet with your law enforcement agency, to get their perspective.

- Review your emergency evacuation and active-shooter policies.
- Consider scheduling an annual Run-Hide fifteen-minute drill.
- Be a shepherd. Take care of yourself first, your colleagues second, and the patrons third. You can only do what you can only do.

NOTE

1. If you want more information about how threat management works, take a look at the Association of Threat Assessment Professionals website at https://www.ATAP worldwide.org. This is a dedicated group of practitioners who have spent their lives and careers working to stop workplace violence, school violence, domestic violence, stalking, and terrorism.

9

The Need for New Responses at Your Library

POLICE OFFICERS AND SECURITY GUARDS

> We need a new way forward. We will always need the police to come to the library, but not always. We need to use other resources and call the police when there are clear signs of impending danger, violence, injury, or weapons.
>
> —Dr. Steve Albrecht

Notice the title of this chapter is not "Welcoming the Police with Open Arms Every Single Day in Your Library," and that's intentional. Based on recent events in 2020 and before, some library employees have strong feelings about having the police respond to their library, even if the police have the best intentions of helping a serious situation.

It is statistically accurate to say a large amount of violent and nonviolent crimes are caused by a small percentage of the population. This is true for drug sales and drug use as well. And to quote criminologists, "Crime is a young man's game," meaning young and male is the most common contact point between people who commit crimes and the police who want to stop or arrest them. There are not a lot of sixty-year-old burglars, twelve-year-old heroin addicts, fifty-two-year-old gang members, or female bank robbers. There are exceptions to every rule, but this concept is true on its face.

One of the primary functions of the police—and one that may have the most common connection to your library—is to keep and preserve the peace. When I was a young police officer in San Diego, California, in the 1980s, we had just switched our department motto over to "To Protect and Serve." That one is fine, but I liked our old one even better: "Your Safety Is Our Business." "Protect and Serve" sounds fuzzy and imprecise when compared to "Your Safety Is Our Business." In the Library World, keeping staff and patrons safe is everyone's business.

In past times, one of the running jokes when cops described their job was that it was often like "armed social work." Police officers get sent to a wide variety of community problems, many of which are outside their area of expertise. This includes ongoing conflicts and civil problems between neighbors, truant teenagers, mentally ill family members in a home, and business disputes that turn threatening. Police officers only have a limited number of tools in their tool kits, between what they carry physically and what they have been trained or told to do by their agencies, their bosses, and the various municipal, penal, juvenile, and drug codes used in their profession. As psychologist Abraham Maslow so accurately put it in his 1966 book, The Psychology of Science, "I suppose it is tempting, if the only tool you have is a hammer, to treat everything as if it were a nail."[1]

I was giving the keynote speech at a large library conference on the East Coast. In my talk, I spoke about the value of calling the police for those situations with patrons who become dangerous, threatening, get out of control, or are simply beyond the service and communication expertise of the library staff or supervisors.

A woman approached me, and I could tell she had "That Look" in her eyes. She said, in a strong tone, "I would never call the police to come to my library!" I said, "Oh? Why is that?" She said, "Because they kill people." I said, "Surely you don't mean that? The police don't kill people at the library. They are there to try to help keep everyone safe and to help get a handle on dangerous situations." She said, "No, they are there to kill people." I told her we would have to agree to disagree, and she walked away. How could I have possibly answered what she said to her satisfaction?

In my Perfect Library World, we would have a relationship between the local Police Department (PD) or Sheriff's Office (SO) that matched Goldilocks and the Three Bears: not too much of them, not too little of them, just the right amount and response from them.

Can we consider liaison opportunities, where officers and deputies and/or the command staff or chiefs or sheriffs just come to say hello and greet staffers and the public, in an informal coffee hour? Can PDs/SOs work with libraries to put on shared community events, like an informational job fair to help with officer/deputy recruitment, or an "Ask a Cop" program, where citizens can talk to cops about legal issues, why they respond the way they do, and what the job is all about, or a program about the dangers of fentanyl in our communities and what parents can do to keep their kids safe?

These are all attempts to build or rebuild community trust, humanize the police, get them out from behind their sunglasses and tactical vests and be part of the community they live and work in too. Patrons can learn, and maybe a few staff members can get a better opinion of the police, too.

PUZZLED ABOUT THE POLICE RESPONSE IN YOUR LIBRARY? PERHAPS A BETTER UNDERSTANDING OF THEIR UNIQUE CULTURE WILL HELP

You may have seen the police come into your library or have responded from their desk inside the library and have not been pleased with their methods. It's also possible that you have seen the police respond to incidents, ranging from a serious, life-threatening situation to a low-risk call for their services, and have been happy with the results. As a taxpayer and an employee, you have every right to question the methods of how police do their work. Are they being fair, legal, ethical, and safe? Are they treating people with empathy who are out of control, and not taking things personally? Do they make arrests with the least amount of force necessary, to keep the arrestee, themselves, and the public on the scene as safe as possible? The old saying, "No one hates a bad cop more than a good cop," has never been more relevant than today.

Most people get what they know about cops and their methods from TV shows and movies—not always the most historically accurate resource, to be sure. Perhaps it would help your understanding of how the police function—in your library and in your community—by getting a better sense of their work culture.

Every profession has a collection of behaviors that contribute to its workplace culture. Some of these are learned by new employees as they start the job, just by what they observe. Others are taught to new employees by longtime employees, who say, "Here's how we really get things done around here." Some workplace cultural norms are defined in the policies and procedures manual; others are expressly transmitted to all employees by the leadership team (or through the company or agency lawyers).

Some workplace cultural traditions are deeply ingrained, going back decades, to when the business or profession was first founded. (Librarians know why a barber pole sign outside the barbershop has red stripes.)

Some workplace traditions weren't illegal or highly inappropriate "back in the day," but they certainly are now. This includes pranks, hazing, bullying, sabotaging someone's work, sexually or racially themed attacks, or trying to drive certain people (most often women and minority applicants or employees) out of their jobs.

All five military service agencies (Army, Navy, Air Force, Coast Guard, Marines) have long-standing traditions. (The Space Force is too new to have any.) Some of these come with rituals, rites, and elaborate ceremonies. (Your Homework Assignment: Ask any current or former Navy sailor what event took place when he or she crossed the Equator at sea for the first time.)

Bankers have a workplace culture, as do truck drivers, airline pilots, lawyers, hairstylists, and even librarians. They all use jargon, slang, and coded language unique to their professions as a way of communicating quickly and effectively with each other.

The Need for New Responses at Your Library

Now imagine that your work culture told you from Day One on the job that "You could be killed while trying to protect the people you serve. Cops die in spectacularly bad ways, every day, mostly in shootings and car crashes. By the way, welcome to the Police Academy." This is what happens, even today. Besides a military basic training / boot camp experience, I can think of no other profession that indoctrinates its new members this way. Officers and deputies are taught constantly to think about "Officer Survival," and that "Hands Kill," on every call they go on or every stop they make.

Consider how that influences their interactions with people, most of whom are not posing a threat to them. "Because of our uniforms and badges, everyone already knows who we are and why we are there. We usually know almost nothing about the people we encounter while doing this job." There is a fear of death or injury that accompanies cops every time they leave the safety of their stations. There is always at least one gun—their own—at every place they go. This creates a mind-set that affects how they work.

On that happy note, consider this list of factors that make up the police culture. Maybe if you can see how they look at the world through their own little drinking straw, it can help you see why they act the way they do:

- It's a calling for most, not just a career or a job.
- It's still a male-based work environment; women have to work much harder to be accepted.
- It allows for some hazing of probationary employees. (Much more of that happens in the fire department culture.)
- It's still a paramilitary structure, with military-influenced job titles, ranks, and uniforms.
- It's a job that comes with no small amount of pride, bordering on arrogance, about their chosen career.
- Most cops are fearful of losing face in front of the public, which leads to their need for constant fear control at scenes.
- It's a twenty-four-hour, all-weather business, which means a twenty-four-hour lifestyle (work, sleep, go back to work, respond to calls, discuss work, repeat).
- It's a highly specialized career, with highly screened and backgrounded applicants. It takes a long time to get hired, and the Police Academy is lengthy, hard, and stress based. The first-year probationary employee training process is rigorous.
- It's (too much of an) alcohol-centered culture. (Way more drinking than firefighters ever do.)
- There's a high suicide rate. (More cops kill themselves each year—120 to 250[2]—than are killed in the line of duty by criminals (not in accidents or from COVID)—from 60 to 130.[3]

- "Five-year disease" interferes with the judgment of new employees, who get too salty, too soon.
- Back, knee, shoulder, and neck injuries are a part of the job.
- Constant opportunities exist to witness death or to be killed on the job, or to see coworkers injured or killed.
- There's the ability and desire to make deep and close friendships and work relationships that can last for life. (I have been friends with three of my patrol car partners for nearly forty years.)
- Cops are Lone Wolf workers; unlike firefighters, who work in teams of four to six, much of their work takes place alone. This can lead to depression and a sense of isolation from the community. (People love firefighters; they tolerate cops.)
- There is plenty of peer support, unless you make an unforgivable tactical mistake.
- Cops are always wary of senior leadership. Everyone above the rank of lieutenant no longer remembers what it's like to do "real police work."
- There's a longtime distrust of most clinicians and the need for getting clinical help for depression, suicidal thoughts, PTSD, or marriage counseling.
- There's a need to "pay your dues first" before you can act like a veteran.
- There is more community suspicion and mutual distrust, which leads to a not always useful "Us versus Them" mentality.

None of the above ever excuses the behavior of unprofessional, rude, dismissive, poorly trained, or dangerous officers who arrive at your library. If you're not getting good service from them at your library, it's time to call the watch commander and have a conversation about what happened and how it needs to be better.

But, if you are truly empathic about the needs of your patrons, can you also be just as empathic toward the police officers or sheriff's deputies who come to your library, with the primary intent of protecting (themselves and you) and serving (you and the patrons)? A little understanding of how their culture orients their worldview can help you understand why they do what they do.

WHEN DO WE NEED A POLICE RESPONSE IN OUR LIBRARIES?

This list is far from inclusive, but it does see the criteria I'm hoping nearly every librarian would agree to, that the police are needed for events that put themselves, the patrons, the facility, and the most valuable materials at risk of harm or theft. Each of these, with a few exceptions like a bomb threat, is going to need to be a 9-1-1 call. Be ready for an assertive police response because this is when they need to do what they do:

- An active-shooter event.
- A person armed with a deadly weapon (gun, knife) threatening or robbing others.

- A fight between two armed patrons.
- A person destroying library furniture, smashing equipment, breaking windows.
- The attempted or actual sexual assault of a patron, child, or employee.
- Attempted or actual kidnapping of a child or an adult.
- Finding a real gun or a large quantity of drugs in the library.
- A violent confrontation between rival gang members.
- Domestic violence, involving a patron or an employee, especially with injuries.
- Hostage or barricaded subject situation—a SWAT call.
- Person(s) trying to steal expensive items or equipment from patrons, staff, or the library.
- Violent crimes happening in the parking lot.
- Bomb threat? Usually only if a suspicious device is found.
- Indecent exposure or possession of child pornography.
- Violation of a Temporary Restraining Order (TRO), where the target is a patron or staff member and the perpetrator is still on scene.

WHEN MIGHT WE NOT NEED A POLICE RESPONSE TO OUR LIBRARY?

If you review these next possibilities and decide you still want to call 9-1-1, that's perfectly fine with me. (Better to call them and not need them than to need them and not call them.) Some of these situations might need a police response later, to help a patron who discovers he or she has just become a crime victim and to take a report. It's always useful to know the non-emergency number for the local PD or sheriff. (Put it into your cell phone contacts.)

- Petty theft of the library's or patron's items.
- Mentally ill or drunk/on drugs patron. (Use our communication and service skills to get him or her to leave.)
- Loud, eccentric, rude, disturbing patron. (Same.)
- Drug overdose event. (Paramedics are needed, not cops.)
- Crime case where the victim will (probably) not cooperate with them.
- Patrons arguing with each other. (Ask them to leave, separately, and not to fight inside or outside the library when they do.)
- Found marijuana or a small amount of drug paraphernalia. (Dispose of it safely.)
- Vicious dog? (Ask the patron to leave. Make a report to the County Animal Control, Humane Society?)
- Students fighting (no injuries); truancy issues; child abuse (Call the school directly? Call Child Protective Services / Adult Protective Services to report).
- Patron gets his or her car hit in the parking lot. (They can call.)

As you can see from the count, there are more "call the police" scenarios than "don't call the police" scenarios. Use your good judgment and intuition. If the event unfolds in a way where you would call the police if the same things were happening on your front lawn or in the parking lot of your apartment building, call them. If you and your colleagues mostly agree the police need to come, call them, even if the vote is not unanimous.

WHAT OTHER LAW ENFORCEMENT RESOURCES CAN HELP US?

The larger the department, the more possible resources they can bring to your library. The following are some examples:

Police or sheriff's agencies may have Crime Prevention Units, most often staffed with trained civilian employees who can provide training, facility security surveys, and information on crime trends.

It's common for larger agencies to have a cadre of dedicated community volunteers who provide certain activities and support that doesn't require being sworn. In my former department at San Diego PD, we have trained senior citizens, called RSVPs (Retired Senior Volunteer Patrols) who drive around in marked cars and do vacation checks, write parking tickets (at your library, if necessary), meet with other seniors to check on them, and direct traffic at various events. You may be able to ask the agency to provide this free help at various events happening at the library that don't require a cop but could benefit from an RSVP.

Some agencies have what are called HOT or PERT squads, which stands for Homeless Outreach Team or Psychiatric Emergency Response Team. The first squad consists of specially trained police officers, social workers, mental health clinicians, and homeless advocates, who specialize in contacting and assisting homeless people (not just striving to put them in jail or kick them out of the city) with programs and treatment. The second squad consists of specifically trained uniformed officers who ride in a patrol car with psychiatric nurses, licensed clinical social workers (LCSWs), psychiatric technicians, or psychologists. They spend the entire eight-, ten-, or twelve-hour shift looking for people with mental health problems, following up on previous mental health–related police calls, speaking with family members about their mentally ill relatives, and trying to intervene in situations before the police and the mentally ill come into violent contact with others.

You may be able to find retired officers or deputies to work part-time security positions in the library.

You can always set an informational or an advisory meeting with the Chief's Office, watch commanders, captains and lieutenants, and sheriffs and undersheriffs to talk about the responses, policies, and protocols of their officers and deputies as it pertains to your library.

You can always get help, advice, and information from your agency's Internal Affairs Unit (for officer complaints about poor service), the Professional

Standards Unit (for potential crimes involving police officers), or Police/Citizens Oversight Boards (for general police misconduct complaints and concerns).

CRAFTING THE PERFECT LIBRARY SECURITY OFFICER

Security guards or security officers, depending on what you call them or they call themselves, get a bad rap these days. No one would want to be called a "Rent-a-Cop" or hear "Look! It's Paul Blart, Mall Cop!," but that's the reputation some of them get and earn. Not all security officers deserve this ridicule, of course, but as one of my weary security consultant pals said, after handling yet another use of force incident with an overzealous uniformed security guard, "Sometimes we are protected by people we should be protected from."

There are usually two types of library security officers: in-house or contract. In-house security officers are more rare, but they could be provided by your city, county, or perhaps through the Sheriff's Department. The benefit of this type is that they have knowledge of crime issues in the area and tend to be more responsive (and loyal) because they are also employees just like you. The downside to contract employees is that you may get stuck with an officer who has retired from duty or is a bit lazy and doesn't do much. You can put some pressure on this person's boss (the security contractor) to get them to work harder.

Contract security employees offer their own set of pros and cons. The biggest downside is they are usually horribly underpaid, and as such, we don't get the quality employee we need because the low pay drives the good guards to go to other firms where they are paid better. The best part about using a contract security officer is that if the firm is reputable and hires well, and has a large number of employees, you can request they put another, better-qualified officer in your library to replace a guard who is not doing the job to your satisfaction. One of your duties is to make sure the contract security officer is a good fit with the culture of your library, as it's oriented by your patrons and employees. Is this person a good service provider and not heavy-handed in the security role? Does this person communicate effectively with patrons and staff of different races, genders, and ages? Does this person intervene in patron behavior issues with skill and tact? If not, you have the right to request another officer from the contractor.

Like creating the perfect service-oriented library employee, getting the best use of security officers in your library will take some careful thought, planning, preparation, and discussion, with both library leaders and staff members. It makes good security sense to talk as a group about the benefits of a security officer and how to make the best use of his or her abilities in your library. Then you can meet with the in-house or contract security providers and explain your needs in detail.

In the Security Guard World, it's all about the "Posted Orders." These orders tell the officer what to do, how to do it, where to do it, when to do it, why to do it, and for whom to do it. The Posted Orders are supposed to be the Last Word on their job duties.

The problem is that too many contract officers are placed in library facilities by the security company's salesperson, using the same Posted Orders that they would use for a factory, warehouse, retail store, or other non-library location. You need Posted Orders that are specifically created for your library.

The first step, if you don't have a security officer now or have never had one, is to start with a clean slate about this person's job duties. Sit down with selected staff members, supervisors, managers, and library leaders and brainstorm what you want—in the Perfect Library World—for this security officer to do.

If you already have a security service in one or more of your libraries, it's not too late to make changes to their Posted Orders. Look at what is on file now and seek to make changes. Let's create a list of job duties and responsibilities for your library security officer. You can add, delete, or modify these suggestions to fit the needs of your building, your patrons, and the security concerns of your staff:

- Be visible, in full uniform, at all times while working.
- Be accessible, by cell phone or radio, at all times while working.
- Patrol the exterior of the library building every hour.
- Patrol the parking lot or parking garage every hour.
- Walk the library floor every thirty minutes.
- Check the public restrooms every hour for illegal activities or violations of our Code of Conduct.
- Greet patrons at the main entrance and provide directions, if necessary.
- Interact with patrons as necessary and redirect them to staff for further help.
- Interact with library staff and supervisors about any safety or security issues.
- Escort patrons from the library who have been asked to leave or have been previously banned.
- Check the Computer Lab, Genealogy Room, and staff work areas several times per shift.
- Brief responding police officers to any security concerns; provide an update about a situation as they arrive.
- Pay attention to any medical emergencies and call 9-1-1; provide basic first aid as able.
- Pay attention to any hazards that could result in injuries, fires, or damage to library property.
- Know the evacuation routes and be ready to evacuate staff and patrons to safe locations outside the building.
- Escort any staff members who request it to their cars in the parking lot after the close of business.

These need to be communicated to the site security manager in charge of the contract for your library. These also need to be measured, using observations and reviews, to make certain the things on paper are being done in person. Once you and the site security manager have agreed these are the appropriate Posted Orders (and they are subject to change and modification, as events or needs dictate), this is the standard that all guards must meet if they are to work in your library.

CROOKS AT YOUR LOCAL LIBRARY?

On a final note on the subject of cops, I wrote an article for police officers so they could better understand what goes on in some libraries when it comes to crime or problematic patrons. Please understand the language I used is designed for their eyes and ears. I'll say it again: I wrote this for street police, not library staffers. Read and understand their work culture accordingly.

> Let's describe a place where these types of people go and see if you can guess where it is. This building is visited by gang members, the homeless, the mentally ill, the drug and alcohol addicted, opiate overdosers, pedophiles, gun and knife carriers, thieves, vandals and taggers, dope dealers, child pornography enthusiasts, flashers, gropers, stalkers, and domestic violence perpetrators. If you [said] county jail you'd be wrong. It's the library, and it's actually worse than you might think.
>
> As libraries [evolve] their services for their communities, we see them trying to be more inclusive, open, and accepting of all kinds of citizens, many of whom have specific or special needs. This can include offering literacy programs for people who cannot read or write at a functional level; LGTBQ programs for minors and adults struggling with their sexual identities; immigration support services for undocumented people; story time for little kids, where they learn to read and love books; programs that assist the elderly with computer literacy, their taxes, or other life issues; legal aid services; teens helped with homework; family movie nights; writing and publishing workshops; and local or national author events. City and county libraries put a lot of effort and thought into how they can stay relevant, by providing a living, changing space that is about more than just books and magazines.
>
> Besides the assortment of actual and potential criminals listed [earlier in this chapter], lots of normal and nice people go to the local library: kids with their parents; retired or elderly folks; K-12 and college students doing research or homework; citizens and visitors looking for help and information; teachers and their classes; and people of all ages and interests who want a quiet, safe place to read, use the Internet, watch online videos, or rent DVDs, records, and books. But like many examples in police work, the good people using the library need your protection from the problem people who invade the library.
>
> Sitting in my office nearly 20 years ago, I received a call from a grant-funded state training organization that specialized in library programs. They asked, "Can you teach your workplace violence prevention workshop to people who work in libraries?" I said, "What could possibly be going on in a public

library where you'd need a safety and security guy like me?" [Thus] began my education about what goes on in libraries and who causes the majority of the problems inside them.

As I taught my half-day workshop, "Library Security: Dealing with Challenging Patrons," around the country, I heard so many stories from library staffers about problematic people doing scary, dangerous, violent, stupid, and irritating things, putting the employees and other normal patrons at risk. As you might expect, I always asked about the police response to their libraries for crimes in progress and getting extra patrols. The answers I got back ranged along a spectrum of service and support from "the police or sheriff deputies come if we call them using 911, but they never just come by to make sure we're safe" to "the police or sheriff's department come by on a regular basis. They know us, we know them, they know the problem patrons here, and they help keep us safe."

So in the spirit of making more work for yourself and your beat partners, if you have a library branch in your service area, add it to your list of stops. In my Perfect Library World, a cop or a deputy would visit the library on an irregular basis, saying hello to the staff, greeting the nice, normal patrons, and giving the hard eye to potentially or actual problematic patrons in the building.

You don't have to go [there] every day. Pick a few moments out of your patrol month [where you] come by once a week for a quick walk-through, or twice in one day, or three times a week, [where] you . . . simply say hello to the relieved staff, check the restrooms, walk the exterior perimeter, and talk over any security or crime problems with the leadership team and/or the posted security guard, if they have one.

You'll want to say hello to normal patrons and chase out problem patrons. This could include predatory or overly aggressive homeless people; gangsters who are there to steal, vandalize, sell drugs, recruit, or intimidate others; people who are clearly under the influence and can't control their behavior; and disruptive mentally ill people. You can keep your eye on a lot of people who may have crime on their minds, and your presence there on a random, irregular, occasional basis makes it hard for them to guess when you might pop in.

As a favor to you, I have instructed my library training participants to welcome you, share relevant Security Incident Reports, and [most importantly], allow you to use the clean and safe staff bathroom. Consider sitting in the library at a safe table to write your reports. Use the library parking lot as a place to sit in your car and eat your lunch. Don't just wait for them to call you. In some cities, the library is near the police department and City Hall, so . . . walk across the plaza and start saying hello.

Library employees are well aware [their profession has seen injuries and deaths around this country]. Within the last year, a library manager was shot and killed in the parking lot of her facility by a mentally ill homeless man in Sacramento. This perpetrator had already been kicked out of several St. Louis, MO-area libraries before he made his way west. The director of the Fort Myers Beach, FL library was stabbed to death by a mentally ill homeless man as he opened the branch one Saturday morning this past January.

Many library staffers already know how to initiate the Run-Hide-Fight protocol for active shooters or mass attackers. They've seen the related YouTube videos and been through training classes on active shooters taught by me or other officers or deputies from their communities.

A number of libraries in this country keep doses of Narcan on hand and certain staffers have been trained to give it to suspected opiate overdosers who frequent their bathrooms, book stacks, or other hidden parts of their facilities.

Library [people] try to be as inclusive, helpful, and welcoming to all. If you have a library branch in your work area, get to know [them] and support their efforts to keep themselves and the normal patrons safe and secure from the abnormal patrons.[4]

* * *

We need to create a new way forward, to build a different relationship with law enforcement, and ask them to provide trustworthy, fair, ethical, and safe services to staff, patrons, and citizens.

A note from your pal Dr. Steve: One last thought from me. Want more cops to swing by your library from time to time? Give them a hard key, an access key, or the door code to the staff bathroom. Officers and deputies like to go potty in peace. This is actually a big deal to them. When you're wearing thirty pounds of tactical gear, you want and need a safe place to relieve yourself. They will thank you with a knowing nod as they leave.

NOTES

1. Abraham Maslow, *The Psychology of Science* (New York: HarperCollins, 1966), p. 15.
2. https://1sthelp.org/the-numbers/.
3. https://www.fbi.gov/services/cjis/ucr/leoka.
4. Steve Albrecht, "Crooks at Your Local Library," *POLICE Magazine*, May 30, 2019, https://www.policemag.com/514298/crooks-at-your-local-library (reprinted with permission).

10

A Plan for Library Emergencies

MEDICAL EVENTS, FIRES, AND BEYOND

In his forty years of work as a consulting security professional to many of the world's most important celebrities and business people (Oprah and some bookstore owner named Jeff Bezos to name just two), Gavin de Becker (www.gdba.com) knows of what he speaks. Many years ago, I attended his multi-day threat assessment training program outside of Los Angeles. During that session, he discussed a safety and security hindrance known as "The Myth of No Past Problems (TMONPP)." This concept has stuck with me all these years, and it is an issue in our libraries today.

In essence, "The Myth of No Past Problems" says that "nothing bad happened at the library yesterday, so probably/hopefully nothing bad will happen at the library today." Taken in a broader way, library leaders and employees say aloud or think to themselves, "That bad thing that happened at that not-a-library place over there has never, ever happened over here. Therefore, it's not very likely that it will or could happen here." Just because you have never had a patron go into cardiac arrest in your library doesn't mean you can disconnect and store away the AED (automated external defibrillator) machines, right?

As we must conclude, TMONPP is just a form of denial, written like a college philosophy course logic problem: "Because this hasn't happened before or here, then it won't happen ever or here." Don't buy into this false belief. Don't compare your library to others, except to learn from what the leaders and staffers did right or wrong in certain difficult situations. It should never apply to any security or safety incident in your library that is possible but not likely. That's why we need to be ready for any event.

We don't make predictions to keep ourselves, our patrons, and our buildings safe. We don't use hope as a prevention strategy.

LET'S FOLLOW THE MAGIC KINGDOM RISK MANAGEMENT MODEL

Disneyland in Anaheim, California, and Disney World in Orlando, Florida, are hugely popular tourist attractions for visitors from nearly every country on the planet. In a typical year, Disneyland gets 18.6 million visitors, and Disney World gets 20.86 million. The Disney World numbers jump to 52 million visitors per year if you count its four theme parks and two water parks.[1] That's a lot of people, and with that many humans wandering around—eating, drinking, and buying in the various Enchanted Kingdoms—something bad is bound to happen. And it does.

According to some pals in the Security Departments on both coasts, at least one visitor to either park goes to the hospital with a serious injury every day. An ambulance is parked at each of the park locations, just waiting to take someone to the hospital, and they do, every single day. Imagine that people get knocked unconscious when they fall out of rides while trying to grab a souvenir, break their bones jumping out of rides that are still moving, slip and fall on a discarded hot dog wrapper, get overcome by heat stroke, or have any number of significant medical problems that involve a lights-and-siren run to a local hospital.

What does this mean to us, trying to run a safe and secure library? Simply that Stuff Happens. We can't always predict when bad things are going to happen, but we can prevent them. The Disney Company doesn't look at its visitors going to hospitals every day as a reason to close down because there is liability in running huge public theme parks. It has ambulances on standby because there is liability already built into running huge public theme parks. We can do likewise, and be ready with already prepared policies, procedures, preexisting employee training, liaison relationships with first responders and other support departments or agencies, and the wisdom to know what to do and when to do it.

MANAGING LIBRARY EMERGENCIES: A "THREAT TEAM" APPROACH TO DOING THE RIGHT THINGS

The Chinese symbol for the word "crisis" is a combination of the symbols for danger and opportunity. It would be great to have the latter without the former, which is always our goal, but life is not easy that way; sometimes we get the response lesson only after the event.

Nearly thirty years ago, I coined a phrase—Corporate Self-Defense[2]—to define the idea of "protecting your organization from internal and external crisis problems—before they occur, while they occur, and after they occur." It made sense in those carefree days before active shooters, 9/11, and mass attacks in our country. It makes even more sense and has more importance today as the world gets more complex, more stressful, and occasionally, more dangerous.

We can't manage what we don't know about. Hope is not a strategy. Hope is not a plan. Prior emergency planning prevents poor performance during an actual emergency.

The list of possible safety and security problems that come with operating a publicly accessed building that's open upward of eighty hours per week means a lot of things can happen. We've examined many of them in these pages already. Some library emergencies are rare and manageable; others are rare and catastrophic. Library directors, managers, supervisors, and staff must know their roles in dealing with building fires, active shooters, weather events, plumbing problems, power blackouts or other utility emergencies, invasive pests, parking lot robberies, burglaries, IT attacks, bomb threats, needle sticks, first aid events, car accidents in the parking lot, slips and falls, protests inside and civil unrest outside, and media management concerns.

My security colleague in North Carolina, Patrick Fiel, is the former chief of security for the Washington, DC, school system. He was in that job before, during, and after the 9/11 attacks. He says, "The main ingredients to an emergency plan are prevention, preparedness, response, and recovery. Your communication plan is a critical part of keeping everyone informed. You must stay consistent in your messaging."[3]

And all that starts with a team-based approach to the internal and external threats that a library may face. There are lots of labels we can use to define the safety and security stakeholders who must get together—coming from inside and outside the library—including other related city or county employees. I have seen the terms "Library Crisis Management Team," "Library Critical Incident Response Team," and "Library Threat Assessment Team" used synonymously to describe the coordinated actions of these groups. As always, business labels don't matter; actions do. What you call your team is not as important as having one, even if it is loosely organized and not formally structured. Depending upon the size of your facilities or library district, you may have to have one or two team members play more than one role.

Here are the usual team members who play the role of being "safety and security stakeholders" for the library. When there is an event that is threatening or could threaten the safety of the staff and patrons or the operation and business continuity of the library, we can gather these people together, in person, or electronically, to brainstorm and come up with a response plan that the majority of the group can agree upon. Your team should be able to call on these colleagues for all serious safety and security challenges:

- Library director or her/his designees
- Human Resources Department / personnel manager
- City attorney / county counsel / town attorney
- Security manager (if that function exists)
- Employee Assistance Program (EAP) provider
- Risk / safety manager (if that function exists)
- Law enforcement liaison
- IT manager

A Plan for Library Emergencies

- Facilities/Maintenance manager
- Public information officer
- Union representatives (if that function exists)
- Other outside services or consultants

We may not need all of these folks gathered in one room all at once, but we can call on the most relevant people, with the most useful expertise and experience, for guidance before we decide how to respond. I consider myself a fairly smart guy, with a lot of expertise and a background in crisis response and crisis management. But I am always smarter when I work in a team, synergistically, to call on all the other IQ points gathered near me.

MEDICAL EMERGENCY IN THE LIBRARY

While fires may be rare, medical emergencies are much more common. I think about first aid events in the library and I'm back to the conversation that I've been having for several years now about the value and the need for more tourniquets. Tourniquets save lives in bleeding events, and there is more likelihood for those than you might first believe.

I've seen tourniquets be very useful for things like parking lot accidents, where somebody got hit by a car or a child fell from some high point, like a staircase, or where they may have a lot of bleeding from a serious cut. There could be any situation involving a gunshot or a knife wound where a tourniquet would be useful. Typically paramedics are going to respond to do that, but in some situations, you may be in a rural location not that accessible to medical care, so knowing how to use a tourniquet will be valuable. Watch YouTube videos on this and also get some instruction from the people who make these devices. The average tourniquet, the good ones, that have a windlass tightening bar and a locking strap, cost about $10, and you can get them on Amazon. They need to go inside lots of library first aid kits.

I think about library-related first aid events with two of our most vulnerable populations: children and the elderly. How do we get our elderly patrons outside? Might you have to carry them down a flight of stairs in a building with no elevator, or carry them to the elevator, or place them in a rolling office chair and wheel them out if they don't have their own wheelchair? I think about the elderly patrons who are vulnerable to being bumped or knocked down, where they can get serious orthopedic injuries.

Children are a whole other concern in the library space. Kids jump off tables, ride carts until they crash, fall down the stairs, or do something inside the library that involves either their own accident or horseplay, where they can get serious head or orthopedic injuries. How do we take care of those kids until the paramedics arrive? These are all part of your discussion about possible worst-case events that could never happen in the library or could happen tomorrow.

We need policies and solutions and a level-headed type of thinking about these rare but possible events before they happen.

For medical emergencies, you should only do what you know how to do. For your own peace of mind and to help others and yourself, you should have a basic knowledge of first aid procedures, and know where the well-stocked, accessible first aid kits are stored in your facility. You should take either a basic CPR class (where you learn to do chest compressions only, on a potential cardiac arrest victim), a more advanced CPR class (where you learn to give mouth-to-mouth resuscitation and chest compressions), AED training (if you have an AED on site), and even so-called "Stop the Bleed" training to know how and when to use tourniquets on yourself or others. (Go to www.stopthebleed.org/ for more information.)

But just as no law demands that you provide first aid to someone in need, you cannot be sued successfully for doing your best in a medical crisis (otherwise known as the "Good Samaritan Law"), unless you acted unreasonably, dangerously, or made the situation much worse. This should make it easier for you to take action to try and save someone's life.

As with a fire in or around the facility, know when to help, and when to help the first responders by clearing out of the area, offering the victims comfort, or providing the first responders with additional information, support, or use of the facility. Be ready to move people to an area inside or outside the building where they can be treated. Discuss with your colleagues how to use things like rolling chairs or blankets to help move injured employees or patrons.

FIRE EMERGENCIES

Your library may never have a fire event of any type in its entire history. Thanks to modern building codes, fire codes, and facility designs, you may never experience a fire, at home or any building you will ever work at. If so, great. But we don't use the absence of one until this point in your personal or professional life as a reason to disconnect the smoke alarms in your house, toss out the fire extinguisher in your kitchen, and not bother to have a fire detection system and water sprinklers installed in our libraries because of no past fires.

The good news is that, if you work in a modern facility, chances are it will have a state-of-the-art fire alarm system, including ceiling sprinklers, smoke and temperature alarms, evacuation procedures, and maybe even a floor warden system. If you work in a historical building, you may not have all of these fire protection features, but overall, building fires in occupied offices, factories, and manufacturing plants are rare. You still need to pay attention and respond to fire alarms, smoke alarms, actual smoke or flames, fire drills, and evacuations.

You are not expected nor required to fight fires or provide medical aid as part of your job; however, safety is everyone's responsibility, especially our supervisors. In some more minor situations, you may be able to do enough to stop the problem on the spot. Examples include helping an employee who has fainted, using a facility fire extinguisher on a small kitchen fire, or getting the facility first aid kit and using the bandages to stop an employee or patron's minor wound.

Remember: When you call 9-1-1 from your cell phone, you may reach a state police dispatcher. You will need to tell them to transfer you to the Fire Department in your area.

When it comes to any fire, if you have even the smallest doubt about your ability to extinguish it, get yourself and everyone else out of the library.

It's not the flames that kill or incapacitate people; it's the smoke inhalation. Evacuate all employees and patrons, call 9-1-1 from a safe location, and stay away from the building until you're told by uniformed fire personnel it's safe to enter.

Once all employees leave, they should never go back inside until it's safe to do so. Smoke kills more people than fire. You can always get another laptop, purse, or cell phone.

You should already know where the safety equipment is for your facility. This includes fire extinguishers, flashlights, first aid kits, smoke alarms, facility maps, and the fire alarm panels.

You should also know how to get out of any part of the building. Your usual escape routes posted on your emergency floor plans may be blocked by smoke, fire, or fallen debris. It's not important how you get out, just that you get out. Break a ground-floor window if you have to. Meet at a predetermined place far from the building where you can be medically assessed and counted.

LIBRARY SUPERVISOR RESPONSIBILITIES FOR MEDICAL AND FIRE EMERGENCIES

Be ready to help evacuate all employees and visitors from any fire situation that appears to be spreading out of control.

Know your limits when it comes to fire or medical emergencies. Only do what you know or have been trained to do. It helps to know who has certain medical skills and certifications among your employees.

Remind all employees about the location of the safety equipment like first aid kits, earthquake kits, blankets, and chemical cleanup stations.

Establish a quarterly walk-through process, where you take all employees in your department to the locations of the safety equipment and evacuation points. Consider this step as part of any new-employee orientation as well.

Remind all employees that, for any situation requiring an evacuation, they must get out of the facility any way they can. They should meet at a predetermined staging location for building fires only, not for active-shooter events.

For serious-injury situations, focus on the needs of your employees. After the situation and scene have stabilized, be a good professional witness and gather information for either the police or your organization's safety and security stakeholders to assist in their investigations. The first twenty-four hours are often the most crucial information-gathering moments, especially if the incident has the potential for litigation. As we know the lawyers like to say, "If you didn't write down what you did, it didn't happen."

WHAT A FIRE CHIEF WANTS YOU TO KNOW ABOUT PREVENTING LIBRARY FIRES

On February 18, 2020, two thirteen-year-old boys allegedly lit a fire in the Children's Section on the top floor of the two-story Porterville, California, library. They fled, as did the other patrons and staff in the building, who all got out safely. Unfortunately, two Porterville firefighters, twenty-five-year-old Patrick Jones and thirty-five-year-old Raymond Figueroa, died while fighting the blaze. The two teenagers, who were released in August 2020 to home confinement, face charges of conspiracy, murder, and arson that could put them in the California Youth Authority until they are twenty-five. The library housed seventy-seven thousand books and was built in 1953; it did not have fire sprinklers.

According to a story in the February 19, 2020, edition of the *Sacramento Bee*:

> For two decades, the city of Porterville discussed the need to upgrade its 67-year-old library where two firefighters were killed Tuesday. The structure was so old it lacked the fire sprinklers required in modern buildings and had numerous other structural problems, according to city officials. A library assessment commissioned by the Porterville City Council in 2008 said that the building whose original floor was built in 1953 "is in relatively good shape," but several repairs including a fire-reporting system "must be addressed." The report recommended a smoke alarm system directly linked to the fire department central station. "With the renovation, a fire-safety upgrade is required," the report says. "A smoke alarm system with central station reporting is a good inexpensive solution. Its estimated cost is $25,000." It's not clear if any of the fire alarm upgrades were made following the 2008 report. The library is so close to a fire station that the risks seemed minimal, said Edith La Vonne, the chairwoman of the Porterville Library and Literacy Commission. "The back wall of the library butts up against Fire Station 1," La Vonne said. "They're just around the corner, so for me the proximity to the fire department . . . I happen to know they're extremely efficient. They're good. They're well trained and so a fire never occurred to me." The 2008 report noted other problems with the library building. Water had damaged the roof in the northeastern corner and the building's foundation was sinking in places due to being built on poor soil. "Electrical service is maxed out and requires an upgrade," the report said. "The suspended ceiling is not braced for earthquakes. The original 3,824-square-foot building constructed in 1953 was expanded in 1974 to two stories, adding 6,100 square feet to the library, according to the 2008 report.[4]

This tragic story should remind all library leaders and all library employees about our collective need to pay careful attention to a fire as a rare but catastrophic event (like the rare possibility of an active shooter in the library). We need to have written and practiced plans in place and still prepare for an unlikely occurrence. The likelihood of a library fire can be estimated on many factors: staff vigilance about not allowing smoking or watching for signs of arson (especially possible from mentally ill patrons or children); the age of your facility (newly constructed buildings are much less likely to catch fire or burn); the installation or absence of water sprinklers, smoke, and heat sensors; a building-wide fire alarm system with audible alarms and a public address system to be used to notify all staff and patrons to evacuate; and the proximity of the fire department and its number of staff.

This last issue is the most surprising to people. According to a 2014 report from the National Fire Protection Association (NFPA), about 70 percent of America's firefighters are volunteers, and 85 percent of the nation's fire departments are all or mostly volunteer. The smallest communities—those with fewer than ten thousand residents—are almost always served by volunteer departments.[5] The majority of fire stations in the United States are staffed by a full-time, paid fire chief and one to three assistant or battalion chiefs; the rest is made up of volunteer firefighters. For rural libraries, there may be a substantial distance and delayed response time by an all-volunteer Fire Department.

As library leaders consider the vexing issue of a building fire, they should discuss and verify the following:

- Marking locations of evacuation routes, for patrons in the front and employees in the rear.
- Moving children, elderly, or disabled patrons out of the building, quickly and safely.
- Having more than one fire drill per year (follow our K–12 schools, who do several).
- Being vigilant of any hazardous materials (hazmat) in storage areas, janitorial closets, kitchens, or break rooms.
- Keeping all gas, electrical, utility, and IT server rooms secured.
- Being aware of any potential chemicals or flammables on site.
- Being constantly aware of children or teenagers playing with lighters or matches.
- Reporting any arson threats or attempted arson by disturbed or disgruntled patrons, of any age, to the police.
- Being vigilant to enforce "No Smoking" by patrons (cigarettes, pipes, cigars, and vape pens).

For professional advice on this issue, I consulted with my colleague, Robert May, JD. Bob is not only an attorney but also a former fire chief for two southern California agencies. He teaches fire leadership and emergency operations management for various fire administrations in the state of California. He is the CEO of Mainstream Unlimited (www.MainstreamUnlimited.com), a firm that specializes in risk management consulting, on-site training, webinars, and site security assessments.

Here are Chief May's thoughts on keeping libraries safe from fires:

Libraries can pose a challenge when it comes to fire and life safety. The buildings are potentially high-occupancy facilities with hidden dangers. Employee and visitor safety are critical. Besides the life safety exposures, the building can house irreplaceable books, priceless valuables, and historical artifacts. It's not uncommon when a library is involved in a fire for the damage to be significant. These buildings pose a high risk to the entity that owns and operates the building, which could be a city or county, a landlord, or a property manager. All libraries must be outfitted to prevent or reduce damage and allow the safe evacuation of employees and patrons.

The first step is to determine the high-risk areas of the building. This would include

- Exhibits featuring highly combustible materials like paper, wood, or textiles.
- Exhibits featuring preserved specimens housed in alcohol or other flammable liquids.
- Tightly-packed rooms with exhibits or bookshelves.
- Rooms housing materials that are easily damaged by smoke, soot, or water.[6]

An important factor in preventing a fire loss is through the maintenance of a good fire prevention program. The fire protection program and accompanying policies need to be in writing and updated periodically.

Management and staff responsibilities need to be defined, and fire prevention procedures need to be established. This program must be based on a high standard of janitorial services, housekeeping, orderliness, maintenance of equipment, and continuous staff training and awareness in both recognizing and eliminating fire hazards (e.g., ignition and fuel sources).

To help in the reduction of these exposures a fire protection plan is needed. According to Chief May, a fire protection plan should have these goals in mind:

- Preserve documents, data, artifacts, exhibits, and equipment.
- Reduce smoke and soot contamination.
- Reduce water damage caused by on-site protection or fire hoses.
- Have a safety plan for the evacuation of staff and visitors.

Chief May continues: "More important than the preservation of the archive and library and its collections is, of course, the safeguarding [of] the lives of its staff and patrons. Life safety must always come first. Library management must ensure that employees know what to do in the event of a fire."[7] He provides the following tips for safeguarding staff and patrons:

- Make sure they know what the building fire alarm sounds like (bells, horns, chimes, speakers with recorded instructions). Fire drills should be conducted at least twice a year.

A Plan for Library Emergencies

- Ensure employees can hear the alarm. Extend alarms to locations where the alarm cannot be heard and make provisions in the interim to alert employees in those areas.
- Ensure all employees know their primary and secondary exit routes. Every archive and library should have an evacuation plan and provide it to all employees. Walk through exit routes to make sure they are clear and available for use. Conditions may change daily due to construction, renovations, repairs, and such.
- Ensure egress paths are not obstructed by such things as storage.
- Ensure exit doors are accessible, unlocked, and not blocked from the other side.
- Ensure exit signs are operating and visible.
- Make sure emergency lights are functional and adequate to illuminate the exit paths in case of a power failure.
- Ensure staff knows where the meeting point is outside the building so they can be accounted for.
- Ensure an introduction to fire prevention is given to all new employees.

Chief May concludes by saying, "No library institution is immune from fire. Library leaders need to ensure they develop plans for dealing with the fire threat. If they do not do it, it places the building and its occupants, visitors, and collections at risk."[8]

Your best ally in the process of keeping your library safe is your local Fire Department. Call the fire chief and/or the fire marshal to set up a meeting and ask for a full inspection of your building. Follow the recommendations—equipment, policies, training, drills—of your fire professionals.

LIBRARY-RELATED EMERGENCIES

Library emergencies are those situations that could be rare or devastating and those situations that could just be simply irritating. As a library director, manager, or supervisor, your function and goal are to keep all staff safe, keep all patrons safe, and keep the facility safe. Some things are built into library facility safety, like fire alarms, burglar alarms, and IT server room alarms, but some things kind of sneak up on us, like bed bugs in the book drop or plumbing emergencies in ancient library restrooms.

When we consider a collection of worst-case scenarios that could ruin your library, it's really based on two themes: the likelihood and the impact. The likelihood of a fire in your facility is quite low, especially if you have a modern facility with smoke alarms, smoke detectors, and a fire control water system with sprinklers in the ceiling. Most modern buildings, with fire doors and multistory water systems are built to prevent the possibility of a catastrophic fire. All that doesn't mean we don't consider it as a possibility (which is why we need a yearly inspection by the fire marshal), just that it's less likely than other facility emergencies.

By contrast, the impact of some library emergencies can range from not that big a deal to devastating. We value human life foremost and must do all we can to protect those people—library employees, patrons, visitors, vendors, maintenance workers, and other city or county employees—when they are inside our facilities. When we open our doors each day, we have what the law calls an "invitee relationship" with people who enter, meaning we have "invited" them inside and our duty of care, like at a retail store, a hotel, or any local, state, or federal government office, is to make sure they have a safe experience. We need to make accurate assessments about the likelihood of an emergency, since we already know the impact is a range of possibilities. As an example, we don't store a box of paper clips in a one-ton fire safe. We do consider, at every moment possible, what we need to do to keep our staff, patrons, and materials safe.

BURGLARIES

It's rare but there is always the possibility of a burglary. If you think about libraries as having computer systems, copiers, printers (color, 3-D, or laser), projectors, TVs, flat screens, laptops, tablets, rare books and ancient documents, art and artifacts, DVDs, old vinyl records, video games, and video game players, that's an attractive collection of targets for most burglars.

The people most likely to break into a library are kids or young adults, about thirteen to twenty-one years old, who are looking to steal some equipment they can use or take to a pawn shop. Consider the amount of collected vandalism that sometimes comes when teenagers get inside a library after hours and the damage they can do. Some of them can be deterred by burglar alarms—which is why I like to post signs around the outside of the facility stating that fact: "Library Monitored by XYZ Alarm Systems."

If this sounds obvious, consider that some libraries don't have a burglar alarm and others don't activate it every night. I'm a fan of burglar alarms; I think they work. I like motion sensors on doors and motion detectors and infrared systems in the ceiling, so we can catch people the moment they step inside the building. An alarm company's response to a silent burglar alarm sent to the police means they're more likely to catch people inside our facilities.

IT DISASTERS

An IT systems hack or a complete or partial failure is a worst-case scenario for libraries. I have seen more than a few ransomware attacks that targeted local libraries. I have seen some articles from IT and cybersecurity professionals saying, "Just pay the ransom and get your server back." I disagree because it only encourages more of these types of intrusions. I understand the wisdom; sometimes people say, "Well, it's just money and we want our system back, so we'll pay up." I think the larger picture is that we need more hack-proof IT servers and better backup systems. If you're a library director and thinking about these issues, get in touch with the best IT people in your city or county, or those IT specialists who are charged with protecting your particular library facility, and make sure they explain how they are vigilant about viruses, hacking, cybersecurity intrusions, denial of service attacks, and ransomware, so it's not as likely to happen.

BOMB THREATS

Bomb threats come and go based on the political and behavioral winds that blow. Sometimes they're more prevalent and other times not so much. We think about bomb threats as being connected to real bombing events that we had in cases like the Unabomber, the Oklahoma City Federal Building bombing, and the Boston Marathon bombing. But in reality bomb threats are hoaxes. I know from my work in workplace violence prevention that bombers make bombs and bomb threat makers make bomb threats. This is an argument I get into a lot with police officers and firefighters. They want to evacuate the building and search for a bomb. I try to tell them that's it's not a great idea because it sends a message to the bomb threat maker that he or she can shut us down with a phone call or an e-mail or some other sort of cryptic way, just by suggesting there's a bomb in the building.

What I typically do in phoned-in, e-mailed, or social media–posted bomb threat situations in libraries is to look for any kind of disgruntled patron, ex-employee issue, or a domestic violence incident involving one of our employees that may have spurred this type of threat. Then I ask the library managers and supervisors to do a cursory search of the building, inside and out, to see if there's anything that even remotely resembles a suspicious package or device. In that rare case, we would call the police and fire departments and evacuate the facility, but otherwise I do not recommend evacuating the library based on a verbal or written threat.

When people hear me say that (police lieutenants, fire chiefs, and some library leaders), they wrongly conclude I don't care about keeping the staff, patrons, and the building's contents safe. Of course I do. I've spent my entire adult life trying to keep people safe and I look at each bomb threat situation based on the reality that most often bombs that go off did so when there was no warning before the bombing. If you look at the above-mentioned Oklahoma City, Boston Marathon, or Unabomber bombs, no bomb threats were made before these explosions. So when I hear about a bomb threat it's always a hoax designed to disrupt the operation. It's typically done by a kid, somebody who is mentally ill, or someone who wants to get revenge against the library system, and they do this as a way to disrupt things. I would say calling the police and the sheriff is a good idea to make a report. After all, making a bomb threat is a serious crime, and the cops may know of other cases at other facilities around town, involving the same perpetrator. But I wouldn't summarily evacuate the facility unless we found a suspicious package or device.

WEAR YOUR CHICKEN LITTLE HAT WITH MORE DIGNITY

When we take a realistic look at emergency situations in libraries, it's easy to be called out as Chicken Little, where we always cry that the sky is falling and none of the stuff that we "predicted" (or more likely, said was possible) ever happens. In my Perfect Library World, that would be great. I don't want anything bad that we've talked about ever to happen, but I also want you to be prepared and think about the things that you need to pay attention to, especially if you're in a leadership position in your library.

And if you're a library employee, you can contribute to our knowledge of safety and security if you see or hear things you think maybe your boss or coworkers have missed. If you see a hazard or a situation where there may be something that's broken or could put somebody at risk of falling, hurting themselves, or becoming a first aid event, you need to speak up. We're all in charge of safety and security; it's not just the responsibility of one designated employee. We may think our bosses are supposed to be everywhere and see everything, but that doesn't happen. We ask all employees to be the eyes and ears of our facility so you can help us identify every safety or security issue.

Even our patrons can see things we don't. They may discover a hazard or even a crime in the corners, in the stacks, in a restroom, or someplace that we're not necessarily looking at all the time. As a Library Safety and Security Guy, I appreciate any kind of input and information I can get from the patrons and the staff. When I think about worst-case scenarios, let's keep it that way, rare but preconsidered and well managed. Because we live in a real world and liability happens the minute we open our doors to the public and our employees, we've got to have our responses ready.

NOTES

1. https://www.statista.com/statistics/194247/worldwide-attendance-at-theme-and-amusement-parks/.
2. Albrecht, Steve. Crisis Management for Corporate Self-Defense. AMACOM Books, 1996.
3. Patrick V. Fiel, Sr., personal interview with author, July 1, 2021, Wallace, North Carolina.
4. "Porterville CA Library Needed Fire-Safety Upgrades for Years," *Sacramento Bee*, February 19, 2020, https://www.sacbee.com/news/california/article240433646.html#storylink=cpy.
5. Madeline Bodin, "Volunteer Fire Departments Are Struggling to Retain Firefighters, While 911 Calls Are Surging," Government Technology, June 29, 2017, https://bit.ly/38cfWbL.
6. Chief Robert May, personal interview with author, April 22, 2022, Burney, California.
7. Ibid.
8. Ibid.

Appendixes: Additional Security Tools

APPENDIX A: SAMPLE SECURITY INCIDENT REPORT FORMAT

APPENDIX B: INSPECTION DAYS

APPENDIX C: THE NEED FOR A VISITOR/VENDOR ACCESS POLICY

APPENDIX D: THE PERILS OF THE PARKING LOT

APPENDIX E: SAFE LIBRARY EVENTS: THE NEED FOR A WRITTEN EMERGENCY PLAN

Appendix A

SAMPLE SECURITY INCIDENT REPORT FORMAT

Security Incident Reports (SIRs) serve many purposes for library leaders and the staff. Their existence can help library directors prove the need for security improvements, ranging from equipment installations to policy changes and from training monies to helping law enforcement see why they may need to step in and address certain violent or repeat offenders among problematic patrons. They can also help library leaders convince elected and appointed officials as to why the library needs security equipment improvements, new or updated policies, or training. Your agency lawyers—city attorney, town attorney, district attorney, for example—will want to read them, as will your municipal insurance provider.

Your library may use a SIR as a catchall report, covering a lot of events, or it may have a separate Safety Report as well, for things that don't specifically involve security/patron behavior issues. With either type of report, it's important to document all incidents and near misses, which describe something that might have happened but didn't. This means we don't wait until there is a situation where someone has been hurt, or wait to say something to someone when we see something that could cause an injury. You can either send someone to get qualified help or post someone near enough to the hazardous situation while you go for help. In other words, don't leave a potentially bad situation unaddressed and hope someone else will report it. Examples include having a coworker stand by a slippery spill while you go get some cleaning materials or standing by a faulty elevator door while a colleague goes to call a maintenance or facilities supervisor. Or a child is running in the library and trips over a big hole in the main hallway rug and almost falls, but catches himself. The rug hole has been there for months with no issues, so no one has paid it much mind. The child almost falling—and the accompanying SIR—can stimulate the need to get it repaired or replaced immediately before the next person does trip, fall, and gets injured.

Speaking of falling, consider how a Safety Report can document what happened at that moment and serve to protect us later. An elderly female patron falls on the staircase between floors and injures her back. She is discovered by another patron, who notifies a staff member, who calls the paramedics and they arrive. As she is loaded into the ambulance, she tells the staff and the paramedics, "I am fine and it was my clumsiness that caused me to fall. I'm embarrassed that this happened. I feel fine, really. This is all a big fuss over me tripping over my own two feet. I'm sure I'm not injured." She says this often enough to even convince the paramedics that she doesn't need to go to the hospital and she'll seek her own medical attention if she needs to. They release her to herself and drive off. She heads home, apologizing for the whole thing as she leaves.

Write the Safety Report to include all of the above details, especially what she said, verbatim. Because two months later, the library will get served with a civil suit from her personal injury attorney, claiming negligence.

What we document in our security and safety reports, when it happened, is valuable. What we wish later we would have put into those reports is worthless.

While there is no perfect SIR form for patron behavioral issues—and yours may look different—there are some major reporting elements that make sense in whatever format is used.

Take what you need from this list to refresh and improve your current SIR. If you don't have an updated form, consider these additional or modified headings when creating a new one.

- Incident Type: Physical, verbal, known person, near miss?
- Incident Details: Who-What-When-Where-Why-How?
- Behaviors and Actions of the Problem Patron: Event details.
- Event History: Background details or causation factors.
- Police Response: Investigations, arrests, reports.
- Fire Department or Paramedics Response: Injuries? Hospitalization?
- Witness Statements: Including valid contact information.
- Environmental Factors: What might have contributed to the incident?
- Evidence: Photos? Documents? Cyber evidence (texts, e-mails)?
- Follow-Up Reports and Actions: Documentation and corrective actions to reduce the likelihood of another incident.

Appendix B

INSPECTION DAYS

Think of all the cool stuff in your library you could be looking at to make sure it's working properly. There are lots of things to be examined to make sure they aren't broken, out of repair, leaking, hissing, sparking, or smoking. Indeed, there are too many things to look at in one day, and you have other important work to do. So do what McDonald's franchisees do and put scheduled inspections on your calendar. Maybe some things need to be looked at every week, every month, every quarter, or once per year. Write them down in January and follow the guidance of your online or paper calendar when those events pop up.

McDonald's certainly knows how to automate things; the company has been telling its business franchise partners what to do and how to do it since 1955. As just one example, McDonald's provides its owners/operators with a book that lays out one (or several) specific maintenance, repair, beautification, or modification tasks every day of the year. Some things happen every day ("clean the bathrooms every two hours") and other things regularly or irregularly. (I'm not sure I want to know when they clean the McFlurry machine and change out the French fry oil, but I'm hopeful it's often.) One example I have seen them requested to do each year is "June 15: repaint and/or restripe the parking lot." Depending on the weather, the number of cars passing over it, and the quality of the previous paint and paint job, it may not need to be repainted. Maybe it's needing just a touch-up or it can be left alone until next year, but the instruction is there to be followed on that day as a reminder.

McDonald's realizes its franchisees are busy people; that's why they try to put everything that needs to be done on a scheduled basis. Here's a partial list you can start with and modify, based on what you have to inspect at your library. You already know you could create a list one hundred items long. Add or subtract from this list and change the frequency as it fits for you. Assign appropriate staff members, or your facilities, maintenance, or janitorial providers to the tasks you can have them do; save the stuff you need to see for yourself.

Get reports back that these items have been inspected and make a note on your calendar:

DAILY

- Inspect the book drops.
- Inspect the restrooms for leaking faucets or toilets, or broken soap or towel dispensers.
- Check the error codes for your burglar or fire alarm panels.
- Check the kitchen or employee break rooms for cleanliness.
- Make sure all "End-of-the-Day" closing procedures are followed.

WEEKLY

- Check your storage areas for blocked aisles, too much stuff in front of the doors, rodents/bugs, water damage.
- Throw out old food from the kitchen or employee break room refrigerator.
- Have staff report any exterior or interior lights that need to be replaced.
- Verify that all camera views are working and that the camera recording system is functioning.
- Get a report from your IT Department or provider about any anomalies in the system (hacking, disruptions, derail of service).

QUARTERLY

- Verify all first aid kits are filled and in posted locations.
- Test any AED (automated external defibrillator) machines.
- Review your employee locker policy; make certain the locks work.
- Test the panic buttons, burglar and emergency exit alarms ("door screamers"), fire alarms, and any fire control devices.
- Inspect all utility rooms—telephone, IT, electric panel rooms, HVAC (heating, ventilation, and air conditioning) rooms.
- Have the backup power generator system tested and make sure there is enough diesel fuel to run it (if you have one).
- Review all money-handling, money storage, and financial instrument procedures.
- Verify that all door locks and all door hardware is in good working order.
- Make certain all potential hazmat (hazardous materials) are stored in safe, lockable locations.
- Review the Posted Orders for the contract security guard provider.

ANNUALLY

- Change the combination to any safe or vault on the property.
- Meet with your Fire Department's fire marshal and your alarm company provider to verify all smoke detectors, water sprinklers, and related equipment is inspected, updated, and working properly.

- Check for valid and installed evacuation maps throughout the library.
- Conduct a fire drill.
- Conduct an active-shooter drill (Run-Hide) with the employees.

Appendix C

THE NEED FOR A VISITOR/VENDOR ACCESS POLICY

When I teach my workplace violence prevention program for my range of public- or private-sector clients, one of the things we discuss is the value and importance of paying better attention to who comes into our buildings and why. If real estate is all about location, location, location, then keeping employees safe at work is all about access control, access control, access control.

One of the examples I use in training to illustrate how things aren't always what they seem when it comes to vendors is a slide featuring a photo of a brown UPS uniform shirt, pants, and socks. The group identifies the uniform as belonging to and worn by every UPS driver they've ever seen. I then tell them I took that picture because I bought that same uniform at a thrift store. The training participants are quite surprised to hear there is no national restriction on buying any kind of uniform. You can buy medical scrubs, military camos, and even patches for a police uniform.

I complicate the UPS uniform scenario even more by asking, "Do you think I could wear this uniform and walk into almost any business pushing a hand truck and breeze right past the receptionist or security guard? Could I get into almost any business dressed this way and no one would ever think to ask me to show my UPS employee ID card? Have you ever even seen a UPS driver wearing an ID card? I've seen FedEx drivers wearing them around their necks, but I can't recall ever having seen a UPS ID."

One of my gym partners works as a UPS driver and he has no specific route. Because he has been with them for only a few years, he doesn't have much seniority and still works as a relief driver. That means he covers for other drivers who are on vacation or sick. He drives a different route nearly every day or the same one for only a week or two at a time. I asked him, since he is not the usual driver for businesses who are used to seeing their same driver nearly every day, does anyone ever ask him to identify himself? No, not once ever, he says. Everyone just waves and goes about their business as he goes about his. He rolls his hand truck into their back rooms and does his pick-up and delivery thing.

Could someone wearing an "official-looking uniform" walk into your library, go back into the employees-only area, and gain access to expensive, valuable, financial, proprietary, or protected items? As a Library Security Guy, this is the kind of thing that keeps me up all night, worrying.

There are certain people we invite to use the public entrance side of our library, mainly patrons. Certain people also use the private entrance side of our library, mainly employees. Then there are those who we permit to come from the public side to the private side. This includes regular vendors—book delivery people, copy machine repair workers, the good folks who refill the soda and snack machines in our break room, FedEx/UPS drivers, janitorial services, and the like. We may have irregular vendors, like maintenance or repair workers, plumbers, electricians, and carpet cleaners. And we may have visitors who are employees of our city or county, if we are connected to a city or town and not an independent, stand-alone library system. This could include everyone from public works employees, facilities employees, IT employees, couriers from our finance office, and regularly scheduled delivery people who work for the same entity as we do.

We could have visits from elected or appointed officials from our own community or neighboring cities or towns; our city attorneys, county counsels, town attorneys, district attorneys, and similar legal people; and our Friends of the Library or Library Board members.

On the public side, it's quite common for library directors or their deputies or department heads to have meetings with patrons. Most of these meetings are cordial and problem free; some are hostile and volatile, based on the high degree of emotionality the patron brings into the meeting room. During one of these confrontational meetings, where the patron starts shouting and won't lower his or her voice or end the meeting and leave the room, I'm certain every director has had that sinking feeling inside where he or she thinks, "I should have met this person out in the library, not here on the second floor, way in the back of the building, where what's happening in my office right now is not heard by anyone."

All this speaks to the need for a Vendor/Visitor Control Policy. We don't need to have every person sign a Visitor Log, but we do need to screen quickly and effectively everyone who comes in wanting to do work, have a meeting, or otherwise go "behind the curtain," from the frontstage part of our business and building to the backstage parts.

Here are our Vendor/Visitor Rules of Thumb:

- All city/county employees (including all library employees) need to wear their visible photo ID while inside your building. This helps to tell employees and patrons who is who.
- All regular delivery people need to be acknowledged and recognized by at least one library employee, who knows them from frequent contact

and can send them into the back. In other words, someone should quickly vouch for them with a hello or a head nod. No vendor should breeze right past and go into our back areas without being seen by at least one library employee.

- No one-time vendors or vendors who come to the facility on an irregular basis should be allowed to enter the back offices or be left alone in those areas without an employee escort. If they need to wait before they can do their work, ask them to wait on the public side of the facility. (Some "salespeople" are not always who they seem, so better safe than sorry.)
- Any visitors—including other city/county employees, patrons, elected/appointed officials—should be asked, in a polite and matter-of-fact way, to sign our Visitors Clipboard. This clipboard should include their name, title, the person they want to see, and when they arrived and left. Since it has been more than twenty years since the 9/11 attacks, this should not be a burden to most people; it is done routinely at many other professional and governmental buildings.
- All visitors need to be walked back to inner office appointments by a reception staff member or library staffer, or met at the transition door (between our public side and our private side) by the person who has the appointment with them.
- All library staffers should be trained and reminded not to bring angry or unstable patrons to meet with senior leaders in private areas. Have them either call the back office to have the supervisors, managers, deputies or assistant directors, or director come out and meet the person, or preferably, to set an appointment to meet the next day. Time heals a lot of anger, and the patron who is irrational and unreasonable today might be much more agreeable twenty-four hours from now.
- Staff members should brief their bosses as to the issue that the patron wants to meet about and give an assessment of his or her levels of anger and cooperation. Any concerns about volatility, now or the next day, should mean that the library leader meets with the patron on the public side of the library and not in his or her office, or even talk only over the phone.
- A colleague can participate as well in meetings with really angry patrons, for "safety in numbers" reasons, and to witness the discussion.

The time to think about creating or updating your Vendor/Visitor Policy is before you have an incident that tells you what you should have done.

Appendix D

THE PERILS OF THE PARKING LOT

Normal people either park their cars in the library parking lot or walk through it on their way to the building. Scary people use the library parking lot for more dangerous, illegal, or threatening reasons.

As the operators of the library building, we also have an extended legal duty to care for the appearance and safety of the parking lot and must pay attention to what goes on there. That doesn't mean you have to move your desk to the parking lot and sit watching what happens, but since the parking lot is the place where our "invitees" (our patrons, customers, vendors, and visitors) make their access to our building, we can't ignore what goes on out there.

There is a concept in the law known as "foreseeability," and while I'm not a lawyer and I'm not here to give you legal advice, the definition is important to us. Foreseeability means "a reasonable anticipation of the possible results of an action, such as what may happen if one is negligent."

In civil cases, this often means we "knew or should have known" something bad, dangerous, or injurious could happen or will happen. Yes, this means we have to be able to predict the future, especially if one or more accidents or incidents would lead a "reasonable person" (and that phrase pops up a lot in court) to believe a crime or an accident could, would, or did happen based on the conditions in the area.

In other words, if there have been a lot of robberies in our library parking lot over several years and a patron is robbed and injured, he or she can sue us (often successfully) by saying we had prior notice of these dangerous events going on and we did nothing to mitigate that risk.

Mitigating the risk of a robbery would mean we have regular patrols by our security officers and local police; we would install bright exterior lights, signs, and cameras.

Of course, installing those anti-robbery measures will not guarantee a parking lot robbery won't happen, but it makes our position much easier to defend in civil court if it does. This goes back to the theme that we recognized problems, took the best steps we could to prevent them, and try to run our business operations by minimizing the likelihood that they could occur.

So, that said, what impression do you get when you drive in and park and walk to the building, especially if you were a first-time visitor to the parking lot? Does it feel safe, inviting, and clean, where a crime is highly unlikely based on the design and who uses the space? Or does it feel unsafe, dark, dirty, and the area has a history of criminal activity attached to it?

One way to know what is going on in your neighborhood is to do an online search for crimes in your neighborhood, or if your Police or Sheriff's Department has a Crime Prevention Unit, the civilian staff can provide crime history reports for your specific address in particular and for your zip code in general. The results—ranging from "We're doing well here" to "Uh-oh"—may surprise you.

The list of potential parking lot safety and security issues is surprisingly long (but not to me, who has seen all of these things outside the library windows):

- car break-ins
- car thefts
- car vandalism
- gasoline thefts
- building vandalism
- drunks and drug users hanging around
- drug sales
- drug overdoses
- medical emergencies
- loud music from loiterers or cars with the windows down
- litter, trash, broken bottles, and used syringes
- graffiti on the asphalt, fences, windows, and buildings
- robberies and muggings
- sex crimes, sexual assaults, indecent exposure
- public urination or defecation
- carjackings
- assaults, fights
- noisy arguments and long-running disputes
- gang activity, fights with rival gangs
- harassment and bullying of patrons or kids by teenagers
- drive-by or run-by purse snatchings
- loitering and congregating to intimidate patrons from using the library
- domestic violence-related fights, assaults
- child-custody disputes during court-ordered drop-offs
- hit-and-run accidents
- car accidents
- car versus pedestrian accidents

- theft of water or electricity from the library
- theft of sprinkler heads, copper pipe, or copper wire
- sleeping in cars during the day and camping overnight
- trespassing through the lot after being banned from the library
- crime casers, preparing to do something

Whew! That is a long list of potential problems. A small number of these issues can be addressed with the right signage, lighting, cameras, and employee vigilance. Most of them will need to be handled by library security officers (if you have them) or by working with the local police or sheriff. Your local officers or deputies should certainly be proactive to address a lot of these behaviors before they turn into crimes. The aftermath of the crimes will require a law enforcement response.

Some safety and security concerns can't be fixed easily or inexpensively—installing new lights and exterior cameras, hiring security officers, and repaving and restriping the parking lot can get costly.

It's important to prioritize any parking lot safety and security improvements based on two issues: likelihood and liability. Misunderstanding or minimizing both can create your pathway to a civil courtroom. Despite what some plaintiffs' attorneys will tell juries about people who work for government agencies, we aren't expected to be able to predict the future, anticipate crimes, or see accidents before they happen. But if we have prior notice of past crimes or accidents, or our list of Security Incident Reports is piled high with parking lot problems, then we can get hammered in court for that classic legal doctrine, "you knew or should have known this bad thing was about to happen to my client."

Our defense of "we didn't have the money in the budget to make security lighting or camera improvements or fix the giant sinkhole in the parking lot before it swallowed up sixteen cars" will fall upon the deaf ears of a judge or jury. They will have expected you to take "reasonable steps that a reasonable library would need to do to mitigate serious risks once they came to your attention." In other words, spend your dollars wisely in the beginning (e.g., repairs, new policies, and security equipment) so they don't get wasted at the end (e.g., civil case settlements and legal fees).

It may help to think of those issues that are criminal or potentially criminal in nature as one category and then consider others that may require a design fix, like permanently blocking off one of the many entrances to your parking lot to improve the traffic flow. Still others may require some outside-the-box (OTB) thinking, so I will note when it's time for some OTB considerations.

Two other suggestions: get help from your safety and security stakeholders who also work for your same city/county (facilities, maintenance, public works, law enforcement, fire, risk management) and borrow/steal good ideas from other libraries who have tamed their parking lots.

- Pay attention to the traffic flow in the parking lot. Note where drivers pick up and drop off people or kids, especially if it's not where it's designated. Be certain the directional signage, painted arrows, and red curbs versus loading zone curbs are visible. Juries love to pay high-dollar amounts in so-called "darting kid" cases, where a child is injured or killed even though he or she ran out from behind two parked cars. Some parking lot designs make this unlikely, and others are more dangerous, with blind spots, frequent speeders, or proximity to an elementary school.
- Consider installing speed bumps if drivers use your parking lot like a race track. These can be especially useful if drivers cut through your parking lot to get to another nearby building, get to an adjacent parking lot, or use it as a shortcut to a major street.
- Install bollards or concrete planter boxes in front of your entrance doors or pedestrian access points. If you need to justify the cost, just Google how many inattentive, elderly, or teenaged drivers mistook the gas pedal for the brake and crashed their cars into the local Starbucks, convenience store, garage, or house. These barriers can prevent people from driving onto your grass, sidewalks, driveways, or into the rear of the building or your loading dock area.
- Install an exterior camera system. You don't need an expensive one, but in these trying times, you do need a system. I get it; banks have cameras and still get robbed. Cameras don't prevent crime; they deter it, especially if you post signs in the parking lot that remind everyone who uses the lot that you have cameras watching what they're doing. At a minimum, your first, best exterior camera should be installed over your main entrance doorway, to see who is entering the library. Other exterior camera views should cover the parking lot and get recorded to a network video recorder (or NVR, to the Cloud). Having any exterior cameras in your parking lot will require an investment in both quality devices and sufficient lighting. You need cameras that can capture nighttime problems, too. (Never install fake cameras as a cost-saving measure anywhere inside or outside the library. We can be liable if someone gets injured and had an expectation that his or her assault was captured on a real camera.)
- Improve your signage. You will need a variety of so-called bailment signs ("Park at Your Own Risk," "We Are Not Responsible for Theft or Damage") to put people on notice; others include "No overnight parking or day/night camping"; "Take all valuables with you, bring your keys, lock your car"; "This area monitored by security cameras" (if that's true).
- Get your security officers outside. They need to leave the library on an irregular schedule (not at the top of each hour, but in a regular, vigilant, but unpredictable way). They can do their security patrols on foot, by car, and by golf cart.

- Meet with your Police Department (PD) or Sheriff's Office (SO). Ask them to do more drive-bys through the parking lot at different times, even when the library is closed; do their reports in the parking lot; exercise their K9s at the nearby park or on the nearby grass if there are any; and focus on the small number of people who may be causing the biggest collection of problems. (When they do this it's called "Problem-Oriented Policing"—or doing POP projects.)
- Talk to your PD's/SO's civilian Parking Enforcement Unit. They may need to drive through your lot on a more regular basis if you are having lots of issues with drivers parking in handicapped stalls without the proper placards or plates, parking in red zone / fire lanes, and blocking loading doors. (Make certain the stalls and curbs are newly painted and have the right signs in place; no need to irritate patrons who get expensive tickets they didn't deserve because it's not fully clear what is legal or illegal parking.) The fearless Parking Ticket Squad can also mark possibly abandoned cars for a seventy-two-hour violation, or verify stolen or stripped cars and tow them away.
- Improve the exterior lighting. Talk with your facilities or maintenance director about getting brighter, more efficient lights in your lot. Some parking lots still use old-school low sodium lights instead of LED lights. LEDs are far superior to the low sodium parking lot lights that many cities and counties installed several decades ago. The low sodium lights are expensive, hazardous when broken, and don't show actual colors of objects at night with any clarity. Have your city or county shops people give you (exciting) lessons on the differences between lumens and candlepower.
- Review Security Incident Reports from the past year. Look for the two things civil suit attorneys love to focus on as a weakness in our security responses: "patterns and practices." This means events that have become a pattern (happening too much) and failed practices (we did not respond or take adequate measures to solve the problem).
- Reward employee vigilance and reporting. Remind all library employees to pay careful attention to what they see as they cross the parking lot. Tell them to watch how and where they come and go to the building before and after work and on their meal breaks. Give your employees an Amazon card every time they report serious safety or crime problems in the parking lot. They see things directors, managers, and supervisors may not see. Praise them for being watchful. The injury or incident they may prevent affects the safety of everybody. Money we don't have to spend on legal claims can be put to good use in the library.
- Remind your public works landscapers or groundskeeping vendors about security vigilance. Tell them to keep all bushes and trees trimmed away from buildings and lights, so as not to provide hiding places or block the view from the street or inside the building. Tell them to report any

vandalism or theft related to sprinkler parts, water spigots, or gas/electrical/telephone utility boxes.
- Tell your maintenance staff to keep the area clean. This may involve them having to pick up broken needles, syringe parts, human waste, and other bloodborne pathogens, so they need to be trained in how to collect and safely dispose of these items. Make certain they are doing their snow removal and sidewalk salting during winter. Have them fix potholes that can damage cars and any concrete- or asphalt-related pedestrian trip hazards.
- OTB Suggestion: Make friends with your (most sober, reasonable, cooperative) Streetwise Frequent Fliers, who hang around the interiors and exteriors of your library. Ask them to police themselves and to help keep the peace in and around "our library." Sometimes street people can speak the necessary language to other street people in ways where the peer pressure can support your efforts to keep everyone safe without needing to involve security or the police.
- OTB Suggestion: Try this if you have overnight sleepers or loiterers who won't leave (and the police can't or won't help). What about doing what convenience stores and gas stations do and play loud classical music through speakers mounted on poles outside?
- OTB Suggestion: Consider installing parking lot gates and lock the gate at the end of the night. This is a big step and it may require discussions, approvals, signage, new policies about cars left inside overnight, legal opinions, and even public comment. You'll also need someone to unlock and lock the gates seven days a week. This should be done by employees from your public works, parks department, maintenance department, or your security guards, not by your library employees.

If you have a large parking lot to secure or your library is adjacent to a multistory parking garage, these can present additional security challenges.

Appendix E

SAFE LIBRARY EVENTS

One of the things that I didn't think about when I was writing my first library security book back in 2015 is the group event. Coming to my rescue is Chet Price, the library safety and security manager in the downtown branch of the Jacksonville, Florida, library. He created a really useful event safety/management form that should be required any time you have a large number of folks coming into your library. You could have a lot of kindergarten kids coming in for a story time session or a magic show, a movie night for teenagers, a well-known guest speaker, or a music concert program involving lots of musicians and their instruments. It could be for an author coming in to speak about his or her new book and that person is more than a bit controversial. Maybe the subject is controversial, and we expect a lot of protesters based on past experiences at other libraries or a conversation with the local police.

Chet's planning form talks about everything from evacuation routes and radios to whether or not we need to have police, additional hired security officers, or paramedics on hand, depending on the number and types of people we expect to attend. We could have an additional three hundred people in the library or just an extra twenty-five. Either way, Chet advises us to look at all the staging areas and where people, like speakers or vendors, will want to set up. All these things to think about for something that may never happen, right? But because we can't predict when a bad thing might occur in our facility, we need to set up guidelines, ranging from quite basic to quite detailed, depending on who will be there. If you have the governor of your state coming to the library, it's certainly different preparations than if you're having a kids' story hour.

Consider if something bad did happen, the plaintiff's attorneys will ask specific, hard questions about our preparation. Did we have a written plan in place? When and who made contact with first responders? Did we have library security on hand, or did we hire additional private security for the event? Was there adequate lighting? These types of things are what the plaintiff's attorneys look at all the time. What we want to have is a response to the rare possibility of an emergency event in one of our gatherings, but we want to do it in such a way that it doesn't interfere with the good times that the participants are having.

If you have 150 teenagers coming off of five school buses, there will be loading/unloading and parking issues. There are ways we want to think about how we'll protect them and the buses coming in and going out of the area. Maybe we need to hire security to direct traffic for some span of time through the parking lot when it's busy. Maybe we have a program designed for our elderly patrons, where some of them may have accessibility and mobility concerns, especially in an emergency. These are the types of things that are addressed in an emergency event plan.

I taught my Library Security program for nearly twenty years before I realized that your library needs a written plan, anytime you host a program for the public or allow a group of adults or children to use your facility. Apparently, I didn't have the brain power to come up with the design for this event emergency plan, since I had to rely on the kindness of pros like Chet Price to give me a copy and allow me to post it for your benefit here.

PUBLIC LIBRARY
EVENT SAFETY PLAN
EVENT NAME

Plan should be sent to <u>Safety and Security Manager</u> <u>45 days</u> prior to your event, and Ensure this document that it is available on-site at the time of your event for quick referencing.

NOTE: The Emergency Operations Plan or elements of it should be activated if any event is out of the scope of the event organizers or staffs abilities to maintain. Person in charge (PIC) should make notifications per Emergency Operations Plan. Person in charge should establish Incident Command until relieved or incident is terminated.

- In the event of an emergency, dial 911

EVENT START DATE AND TIME:

EVENT END DATE AND TIME:

EVENT LOCATION(S):

One time event _____   On-going Event_____

If ongoing event describe frequency and fill in boxes below with estimated averages of attendees. (E.g., toddler reading program every Thursday 10a-12p from Jan thru Dec) (Summer program every week varied presenters from 9a-2p June 1 to Aug 30)

Public Library Safety and Security

Source: Chester Price, Safety and Security Manager, Emergency Coordinating Officer, Jacksonville Public Library, Jacksonville, Florida

EVENT DESCRIPTION

Describe title of event, what the event will entail types of activities expect to occur and if appropriate if it involves large numbers of children.

ESTIMATED ATTENDANCE

Please provide the estimate attendance for your event.

SCHEDULE OF EVENTS

List all major times involved in setup, event operations, and cleanup/teardown.

Date and Time	Event	Location of Event	Contact

COORDINATORS AND STAFF CONTACT INFORMATION

Insert more tables as needed.

Name (First & Last)	Title and Org.	Cell Phone Number	Email

Source: Chester Price, Safety and Security Manager, Emergency Coordinating Officer, Jacksonville Public Library, Jacksonville, Florida

EVENT COORDINATORS LOCATION

Identify a physical location where event leadership or command center will be located during the event. (This might be the manager's office or registration table)

COMMUNICATIONS PLAN

Identify how the personnel working the event will communicate. IE. Two-way radios and/or cell phones.

WEATHER AND OTHER OUTSIDE EVENTS MONITORING

List any persons who will be utilized to track and monitor weather conditions, fires, demonstrations etc.

EMERGENCY NOTIFICATIONS

Shall be as directed in the JPL EMERGENCY MANAGEMENT PLAN please refer to the Building Emergency Action Plan page in the JPL Emergency Action Plan to access building specific information.

SECURITY

Is there going to be security on site for event?_____Start and stop times. _____

Is additional or extra security needed for event and if so how many?_____ Start and stop times_____

OTHER SECURITY CONCERNS SHOULD BE LISTED ON LAST PAGE

MEDICAL INFORMATION

List locations of AEDs, first aid kit, etc.

ON-SITE EMERGENCY PERSONNEL

Will Police, Fire or EMS be onsite and if so how many

Public Library Safety and Security

Source: Chester Price, Safety and Security Manager, Emergency Coordinating Officer, Jacksonville Public Library, Jacksonville, Florida

NOTIFICATIONS

In the event of an emergency or need to evacuate the event below are items to be performed to ensure all persons in attendance are warned and can evacuate.

Emergency notifications	Person Responsible	Contact number
Notify the Event PIC of Emergency/Severe Weather		
Make Announcements		
Ensure Sheltering Locations Are Open		
Direct volunteers/staff, guests out of the event site		
Contact Police or Fire if appropriate		
Other		

HOLD PRE EVENT SAFETY BRIEFING

SAFETY BRIEFING

Name of person giving briefing, topics to be covered, Codes, Evacuation plan, rally points etc.

ADDITIONAL CONTACTS

For additional information contact:

Safety and Security Manager

Source: Chester Price, Safety and Security Manager, Emergency Coordinating Officer, Jacksonville Public Library, Jacksonville, Florida

EVENT MAP

Detailed floor plan map of the event site and the program. This should include placement of tables and chairs, stages, risers and any other event items to be placed on the floors.

Source: Chester Price, Safety and Security Manager, Emergency Coordinating Officer, Jacksonville Public Library, Jacksonville, Florida

Additional Information:

Security OPS: (number and position as well as duties of security team)

Situational Awareness Concerns: (VIPS attending, Threats, Crowd concerns etc.):

Source: Chester Price, Safety and Security Manager, Emergency Coordinating Officer, Jacksonville Public Library, Jacksonville, Florida

Index

12-step programs, 57

abusers, xx, 76–77
access control policy, 143–45
active attackers, 99–107;
   and ALICE approach, 106
   debriefings, 100
   drills for, 102, 106, 141
   and fatalities, xvii, 119
   information leakage by, 100, 101–2
   and Lifeguard Model, 99
   and police, 104, 113
   prevention, 100, 101–3
   and Run-Hide-Fight approach, 96–97, 100, 102, 104–7, 141
   and safe rooms, 85, 92, 93
Adult Protective Services (APS), 24, 77, 114
AED machines and training, 102, 125, 140
age and crime, 109
alarms:
   burglar, 95, 131, 140
   fire, 104–5, 125, 127, 128, 129, 140
   panic, 18–19, 90, 102, 140
Albrecht, Karl, 12, 14, 66
alcohol:
   signs of, 58, 59
   withdrawal from, 39
Alcoholics Anonymous, 57
ALICE (Alert, Lockdown, Inform, Counter, Evacuate), 106
alignment in communication, 9–10, 47, 70, 93
American Library Association, 79
annual inspection tasks, 140–41
apologizing for security, stopping, 18–23
appointments for patron interactions, 10, 145

APS (Adult Protective Services), 24, 77, 114
arson, 127, 128
assertiveness:
   in Essential Eight approach, 2, 3
   and rural/small systems, 86, 92
   and setting boundaries, 31–32, 35, 36
   strategies for, 9, 11, 41, 74
Assertive Whisper, 9
Association of Threat Assessment Professionals, 107
audits, safety and security, 17
authenticity in service, 13
autism spectrum, patrons on, 39, 71, 72, 79–81

bans on materials, proposed, xx, 78–79
bans on patrons, 32, 36, 94
barriers, using, 47, 61
body language, 7–8
bomb threats, 113, 114, 132
books, protests about, xx, 78–79
boundaries, setting:
   and challenging patrons, 70, 74
   and harassment, 30, 31–32, 35, 36
   and homeless patrons, 44, 45, 47
building and physical environment:
   and active attackers, 100
   doors and locks, 18, 19, 95, 102, 140
   landscaping, 151–52
   parking lot, 18, 81, 117, 147–52
   patrols of, 117
   safe rooms, 85, 92, 93
   sightlines and blind spots, 18, 94
bullying, xix, 75
burglar alarms, 95, 131, 140
burglary, 81, 82, 131
burnout, 14, 15, 16

"calm down" phrase, 5-6
cameras:
    maintaining, 21, 140
    need for, 18
    and parking lot, 147, 149, 150
    and rural/small systems, 89, 94
    using footage, 75
carfentanil, 60
casing behavior, 82
challenge culture, 20-23
challenging patrons:
    approaches to, 70-84
    challenging vs. difficult term, 65-66
    coaching up, xx, 12, 66-69
    and Critical Core Ten approach, 4-5, 47
    and Essential Eight approach, 2-4, 66
    evaluating, 69-70
    and Pareto principle, xix, 66
    role-playing for, 23-27, 72
    staff collaboration on, 23-27, 72, 93-94, 145
    and trauma, xviii, 49-50
    types of, xvi, xix-xx, 69-84
    Yes, No, Maybe people, 6-7, 12. *See also* homeless patrons; mental health disorders, patrons with; substance abuse disorders, patrons with
check-in calls, 88-89
Child Protective Services (CPS), 24, 77
children:
    abuse concerns, 24, 77
    as challenging patrons, xix, 75
    and evacuations, 128
    and medical emergencies, 124
citizen's arrests, 83
Civil Rights Act, 30
coaching skills and management, 16-17
coaching up patrons, xx, 12, 66-69
cocaine, 59, 60
Code of Conduct:
    and Critical Core Ten approach, 4
    enforcing, xvi-xvii, 14, 47, 70, 74
    and Essential Eight approach, 2-4
Code of Quality Service, 12-14
code words, 89, 93, 105
common sense, 4, 14

communication:
    alignment in, 9-10, 47, 70, 93
    assertiveness in, 3, 9
    emotions in, 5-9
    humor in, 12, 47
    limiting forms of, 10
    nonverbal, 7-8
    strategies, 5-12, 46-47, 79
    with supervisors before patron interactions, 9-10, 145
community organizations:
    12-step programs, 57
    and rural/small systems, 89, 96
community stakeholders:
    and emergency planning, 123-24
    and homelessness, 46-47
    and parking lot, 149
    and rural/small systems, 86-88, 96
compassion fatigue, 16
complaints about materials, xx, 78-79
computers, library:
    and emergency planning, 123, 131-32, 140
    and homeless patrons, 45
    internet hogs, xvi, xx, 77
    and pornography, xix, 74-75
    software security, 18
    and technologically-confused patrons, xix, 71
concealment, 103
Conditions Red/White/Yellow, 2
confinement and autistic patrons, 79, 80
confrontation, changing the ratios of, 9-10
consequences, enforcing, 70, 83
consistency in Essential Eight approach, 3
Corporate Self-Defense, 122
costs, 18, 22, 88
countertransference, 16
cover, 103
COVID-19 pandemic, xv
CPR, 125
CPS (Child Protective Services), 24, 77
creativity, 5, 14
crime:
    and age, 109
    burglary, 81, 82, 131
    crime histories, 148

and gender, 109
increase in, xvii
and parking lot, 148-49
stalking, 33-35.
See also active attackers; theft
Crime Prevention Units, 115
Critical Core Ten, 4-5, 47
Crucial Conversations (Grenny, et al.), 5, 7
culture:
   challenge culture, 20-23
   in Critical Core Ten approach, 4
   police, 53-54, 111-13
   and security solutions, 17

daily inspection tasks, 140
Dangerous Behavior Triad, 40-41
deaths, xvii
de Becker, Gavin, 121
DEI (diversity, equity, and inclusion) programs, xxi
delivery people and access policy, 143-45
dependent adults, xx, 76-77
developmentally-disabled patrons, xx, 76-77
difficult *vs.* challenging term, 65-66
director, library:
   and emergency planning, 123, 130, 131-32
   gender ratios, 1
   and material challenges, 78, 79
   role in harassment, 30, 31, 32, 33, 34
   role in safety, xvii, xx, xxii-xxiii
   and rural/small system security, 87
disabled patrons:
   as challenging, xvi, xx, 76-77
   and evacuations, 124, 128, 154
Disneyland/Disney World, 122
distance, maintaining physical, 41, 47, 61, 62, 80
diversity, equity, and inclusion (DEI) programs, xxi
documentation of incidents, 137-38
dogs, 91
doors and locks, 18, 19, 95, 102, 140
Dowd, Ryan, 37, 38, 47-48
drills:
   active attacker, 102, 106, 141
   fire, 128, 129, 141

drugs:
   exposure dangers, xviii-xix, 59-60, 152
   overdoses, 52, 59, 60-61, 114
   paraphernalia, xix, 60, 152.
   See also substance abuse disorders, patrons with
duress buttons, 95

eccentric patrons, xix, 72, 73
elderly patrons:
   and Adult Protective Services, 24, 77, 114
   as challenging, xvi, xx, 76-77
   and evacuations, 124, 128, 154
   and medical emergencies, 124
embarrassment, 7-9
emergency medical services:
   and library events, 153
   and overdoses, 52, 59, 60, 61, 114
   and Security Incident Reports, 138
emergency planning, 121-33;
   and active attackers, 96-97, 100, 102, 105-6, 141
   and bomb threats, 113, 114, 132
   and burglaries, 131
   code phrases, 105
   and computers and IT, 123, 131-32, 140
   and fires, xvii, 125-30, 140-41
   "ICE box" for, 94
   importance of, xx, 122
   inspections for, 139-41
   phone number lists, 94
   and safety and security stakeholders, 123-24.
   See also evacuations; medical emergencies
emotions:
   in communication, 5-9
   and cooling-off periods, 10
   about homelessness, 38
   recognizing, 8
empathy:
   demonstrating, 5-6, 70, 74
   and embarrassment, 8-9
   in Essential Eight approach, 3
   and homeless patrons, 37

and material challenges, 78
phrases for, 5–6
Employee Assistance Program
counseling, 36, 103, 106, 123
Employee Quality of Worklife (EQWL)
surveys, 17
employees. *See* staff; training, staff
energy and friendliness, 13
entitled patrons, xvi, xix, 72–73
EQWL (Employee Quality of Worklife)
surveys, 17
escape plans, 91. *See also* evacuations
escorting visitors, 145
Essential Eight approach, 2–4, 47, 66
evacuations:
    and active attackers, 104–5, 106
    and bomb threats, 132
    and events, 153, 154
    and fires, 126, 128, 129, 130
    and inspections, 141
    and medical emergencies, 124, 125
    and rural/small systems, 91
    and security guards, 117
    staging areas, 106, 126
    and supervisors, 126
events and programming, xvi, 20, 153–59
exasperating patrons, xix, 72, 73–74
exits:
    maintaining exit paths, 47
    rear exits, 95–96
    signage for, 130
extinction technique, 67–69
eyes, signs of substance abuse in, 58

fairness in Essential Eight approach, 2–3
fear and stalking, 34
felony theft, 82
fentanyl, 39, 59–60
Fiel, Patrick, 123
fire alarms, 104–5, 125, 127, 128, 129, 140
firearm laws, 95
fire department:
    fire prevention tips, 127–30
    and inspections, 140
    and medical emergencies, 61
    response times, 128
    and rural/small systems, 89, 94, 95
    and Security Incident Reports, 138

fires, xvii, 125–30, 140–41
firmness in Essential Eight approach, 2
first aid kits, 94, 102, 124, 125, 140
first/last thirty seconds, 13, 14
food and drink:
    and autistic patrons, 80–81
    and employees, 140
foreseeability, 23, 147, 149

gates, 152
gender:
    and active attackers, 100, 103
    and crime, 109
    and harassment, xviii, 29–30
    and perception of safety, 1–2
    ratios of staff, 1
Good Samaritan laws, 125
grand theft, 81–83
Graves, Keith, 61–63
greetings, 13
Grenny, Joseph, 5
Grove, Cindy, 57
guardians and autistic patrons, 79–81

hands, Secret Service, 96
hand signals, 93
harassment, xviii, 16, 29–36, 44
Hargadon, Steve, 43
heroin, 59–60
high stakes and communication, 7
homeless patrons, 37–48;
    behavior issues, 40–41, 44–45
    and Dangerous Behavior Triad, 40–41
    increase in, xviii
    and mental illness, 39, 40, 41, 44, 49
    organizations for, 42–43
    and parking lot, 149, 152
    and police, 39, 40, 115
    staff attitudes on, 38, 43–46
    strategies for, 46–47
    and substance abuse, 39, 40, 41, 44, 49
    terms for, xxi, 37–38
    types of, 38–40
    and violence, 38, 44, 53–54
HOT squads, 115

humor, 12, 47
hydrocodone, 57
hygiene, 44, 58–59

"ICE box," 94
indecent exposure, 74–75, 114
information leakage and active attackers, 100, 101–2
In Search of Excellence (Peters and Waterman), 17
Inspection and Control Audits, 17
inspections, 17, 139–41
internet. *See* computers, library
intuition:
    and calling police, 21–22, 115
    and emergencies, 106
    and substance abuse, 59, 61
    trusting, xxiii, 2, 4
investigations, criminal, 34–35
investigative process for harassment, 30, 32–33
isolating patrons, 41
IT department. *See* computers, library

keys, 18, 19, 94, 104

landscaping, 151–52
law enforcement. *See* police and law enforcement
laws:
    and Critical Core Ten approach, 4
    firearm, 95
least reinforcing syndrome, 68
legality in Essential Eight approach, 3
liability. *See* foreseeability; prior notice
The Librarian's Guide to Homelessness (Dowd), 37
Libraries and the Substance Abuse Crisis (Grove), 57
Library Security (Albrecht), xvii, 1
Lifeguard Model, 92, 99
lights:
    and autistic patrons, 79
    parking lot, 18, 147, 149, 150, 151
    and safety, 18, 129, 130
listening:
    and challenging patrons, 76, 78
    as management skill, 17
    and patience, 3, 6
    with skill, 70
locks:
    desk-mounted front door, 95
    inspecting, 140
    need for, 18, 19, 102
    and parking lot gates, 152
lonely patrons, xix, 70

mace. *See* pepper spray
management:
    and challenge culture, 20–23
    coaching skills, 16–17
    data collection tools, 17–18
    and emergency planning, 106, 123, 130, 131–32
    and harassment, 29–36
    and homeless patrons, 46–47
    and material challenges, 78–79
    preparing for patron interactions, 9–10, 145
    role in safety, xvii, xx, xxii–xxiii, 21
    and rural/small system security, 87
Management By Walking Around (MBWA), 17
mandated reporting of abuse, 76–77
marijuana, 58–59, 60
material challenges, xx, 78–79
materials, checking out by autistic patrons, 80
May, Robert, 128–30
MBWA (Management By Walking Around), 17
McDonald's, 139
McMillan, Ron, 5
media:
    and active attackers, 103
    social media monitoring, 102
medical emergencies:
    and Critical Core Ten approach, 4
    overdoses, 52, 59, 60–61, 114
    and parking lot, 148
    preparing for, 124–25, 126
    and security guards, 117
    in Security Incident Reports, 138
meeting points. *See* staging areas
meltdowns and autistic patrons, 79, 80, 81

mental health disorders, patrons with, 49–63;
    assessment criteria, xviii–xix, 54–55
    and body odor, 59
    borderline behavior by, 54–55
    as challenging, xvi, xviii–xix, 52–57
    and Critical Core Ten approach, 4
    defined, 50–51
    and homelessness, 39, 40, 41, 44, 49
    and meth psychosis, 62
    organizations and services for, 55–57
    and police, xviii–xix, 51, 53–55, 114, 115
    reasons for visiting library, 50–51
    terms for, xxii
    and trauma, 49–50
mental health of staff, 36, 103
methamphetamine, 39, 59, 60, 61–63
meth psychosis, 62
modeling. *See* coaching up patrons
motivation, staff, 16
Movement, Physical, 9
multiple channels of reporting and harassment, 30, 32–33
Myth of No Past Problems, 121

name tags, 34
Narcotics Anonymous, 57
needles and needlesticks, xix, 59–60, 152
needy patrons, xix, 70
nonverbal communication, 7–8

OC pepper spray, 54, 90–91
odor:
    and autistic patrons, 79
    and signs of mental health disorders, 59
    and signs of substance abuse, 58–59
opiates:
    and drug exposure risks, xviii–xix, 59–60, 152
    and overdoses, 52, 59, 60–61, 114
    signs of, 58, 59
    withdrawal from, 39
opinions and communication, strong, 7
overdoses, 52, 59, 60–61, 114

panic alarms, 18–19, 90, 102, 140
paramedics. *See* emergency medical services
paraphernalia, drug, xix, 60, 152
parents, angry, xix, 76
Pareto, Vilfredo, xix
Pareto principle, xix, 66
parking lot, 18, 81, 117, 147–52
patience:
    and challenging patrons, 68, 70
    in Essential Eight approach, 3
    and listening, 3, 6
patron feedback surveys, 17
patron interactions:
    appointments for, 10, 145
    coaching up, xx, 12, 66–69
    Critical Core Ten approach, 4–5
    and Dangerous Behavior Triad, 40–41
    Essential Eight approach, 2–4
    extinction technique, 67–69
    and harassment, xviii, 16, 29–36
    preparing supervisors for, 9–10, 145
    Yes, No, Maybe people, 6–7, 12.
    See also communication
patrons:
    restrictions and bans on, 32, 36, 94
    vigilance by, 19.
    See also challenging patrons; homeless patrons; mental health disorders, patrons with; substance abuse disorders, patrons with
Patterson, Kerry, 5
pepper spray, 54, 90–91
Perfect Library World concept, xxii
personal information, protecting, 34, 35, 83
PERT squads, 115
Peters, Tom, 17
petty theft, 81–83
phantom coworker, 90
Physical Movement, 9
Pinsky, Drew, 38, 41
police and law enforcement, 109–20;
    and active attackers, 104, 113
    and bomb threats, 132
    calling, 21–22, 113–15
    and citizen's arrests, 83
    and crime histories, 148

and Critical Core Ten approach, 4
culture of, 53–54, 111–13
and events, 153
and homeless patrons, 39, 40, 115
liaisons, 110, 123
and parking lot, 149, 151
and patrons with mental health disorders, xviii–xix, 51, 53–55, 114, 115
and patrons with substance abuse disorders, 52, 60, 114
resources, 115–16
and restraining orders, 35–36
and restrooms, 119, 120
and rural/small locations, xx, 85, 86, 94
and school resource officers, 75
and Security Incident Reports, 138
staff attitudes on, 109, 110
and stalking, 34–35
and theft, 82–83, 114
volunteers, 115
working with, xv, 19, 109–20
politicians and rural/small systems, 86–88
pornography, xix, 74–75
Posted Orders, 116–18, 140
posttraumatic stress disorder (PTSD), 103
predatory behavior, 40–41
Price, Chet, 153–54
prior notice, 23, 147, 149
Problem-Oriented Policing, 151
problem solving, 13–14
programming and events, xvi, 20, 153–59
PTSD (posttraumatic stress disorder), 103

quarterly inspection tasks, 140
questions:
 and communication, 3
 and Yes, No, Maybe people, 12

racial harassment, xviii, 29–36
ratios of confrontation, changing, 9–10
reasonableness in Essential Eight approach, 3–4
Red, Condition, 2
relationships and homelessness, 39, 41–43

reporting:
 abuse, 76–77
 harassment, 30, 32–33
 Safety Reports, 137
 Security Incident Reports, 137–38
Request for Reconsideration Form, 78–79
restraining orders, 35–36, 94
restrooms:
 and autistic patrons, 79
 and homeless patrons, 44
 and police, 119, 120
 and security patrols, 117, 140
retaliation, 31
Retired Senior Volunteer Patrols (RSVPs), 115
revenge, 101, 132
risk management, 122, 147
robbery pack, 92
role-playing and scenarios, 23–27, 72
RSVPs (Retired Senior Volunteer Patrols), 115
Run-Hide-Fight, 96–97, 100, 102, 104–7, 141
rural and small locations, 85–97;
 and police, xx, 85, 86, 94
 working alone strategies, 86, 88–92
 working with colleagues strategies, 93–97

safe rooms, 85, 92, 93
safety and security stakeholders:
 defined, 87
 and emergency planning, 123–24
 and parking lot, 149
 and rural/small systems, 87–88, 94
Safety Reports, 137
SAMHSA (Substance Abuse and Mental Health Services Administration), 50–51
scenarios and role-playing, 23–27
school resource officers, 75
Secret Service hands, 96
security:
 apologizing for, 18–23
 challenge culture, 20–23
 data collection tools, 17–18
 need for, 16, 18–23
security guards:

Index **167**

and commercial security patrols, 89
and events, 153
and parking lot, 150, 152
Posted Orders, 116-18, 140
working with, 19, 21, 115, 116-18
Security Incident Reports (SIRs), 137-38
security patrols, 89
self-care, 14, 72
service:
Code of Quality Service, 12-14
goals of, 66-67
Service America! (Albrecht), 12, 66
Service Triangle, 12
sexual exposure, 74-75, 114
sexual harassment, xviii, 16, 29-36, 44
sexual predation, 40
shame, 7-9
Shamu method, 67-69
shepherds concept, xvi, 107
shootings. *See* active attackers
signage:
about cameras and alarms, 89, 131
exit signs, 130
and parking lot, 149, 150, 151
SIRs (Security Incident Reports), 137-38
situational awareness, 96
sleeping in library, 44
smoke inhalation, 126
social media, 102
social workers, 42, 55-56
solo working strategies, 86, 88-92
speed bumps, 150
staff:
attitudes on homelessness, 38, 43-46
attitudes on police, 109, 110
burnout, 14, 15, 16
and challenge culture, 20-23
and citizen's arrests, 83
collaboration on challenging patrons, 23-27, 72, 93-94, 145
gender ratios, 1
and harassment, xviii, 16, 29-36, 44
mental health of, 36, 103
motivation of, 16
personal information of, 34, 35, 83
phantom coworker, 90
role in safety, xvii, xx, xxii-xxiii, 20-23, 133

role-playing by, 23-27, 72
rural locations, working alone strategies, 86, 88-92
rural locations, working with colleagues strategies, 93-97
thanking, 21, 22
and trauma, 16, 100, 103
vigilance by, 19, 96, 133.
See also training, staff
staging areas:
and active attackers, 106
and fires, 126, 130
stalking, 33-35
staring, xix, 71-72
stay-away order. *See* restraining orders
Substance Abuse and Mental Health Services Administration (SAMHSA), 50-51
substance abuse disorders, patrons with, 49-63;
as challenge, xvi, xviii-xix, 57-63
defined, 57
and exposure dangers, xviii-xix, 59-60, 152
and homelessness, 39, 40, 41, 44, 49
overdoses, 52, 59, 60-61, 114
and paraphernalia, xix, 60, 152
and parking lot, 148
and police, 52, 60, 114
reasons for visiting library, 51-52
signs of, 58-59
stages of, 58
and trauma, 49-50
and violence, 60-61
supervisors:
coaching skills, 16-17
and emergencies, 106, 117, 123, 125-26, 132
and gender differences in perception of safety, 2
and harassment, 30-34, 36
and material challenges, 78-79
preparing for patron interactions, 9-10, 145
role in safety, xvii, xxii-xxiii, 19, 22
and rural/small systems, 88, 89
and service, 12, 13

Sutherland, Amy, 67, 68
Switzler, Al, 5

technologically-confused patrons, xix, 71
teenagers, xvi, xix, 75
Temporary Restraining Orders. *See* restraining orders
thanking:
    employees, 21, 22
    patrons, 12, 14
theft:
    categories of, 81-83
    deterrence of, 18
    and homeless patrons, 44
    and parking lot, 148, 149, 152
    and police, 82-83, 114
    robbery pack for, 92
    and rural/small systems, 92
    strategies for, 81-84
third-party leakage, 101-2
thirty seconds, first/last, 13, 14
Thompson, George, 5, 6, 11
tolerance, drug, 57
tourniquets, 94, 102, 124, 125
training, staff:
    and Code of Quality Service, 13
    in CPR and first aid, 125, 126
    and data collection tools, 17-18
    for emergencies, 125
    need for, 15-17
    of new employees, 16, 126, 130
    with role-playing, 23-27, 72
trauma, xviii, 16, 49-50, 100, 103
trauma-informed care, 50
Triple-E patrons, xix, 72-74
Trott, Barry, 78-79

vandalism, xvi, 131, 148, 152
vendor access policy, 143-45
venting, allowing, 70
Verbal Judo (Thompson), 5, 11
Verbal Judo Institute, 5
Veterans Administration, 56
victim *vs.* target term, 29
vigilance:
    and fire safety, 128

    and parking lot, 149, 151
    by patrons, 19, 133
    by staff, 19, 96, 133
violence:
    and autistic patrons, 80
    and homeless patrons, 38, 44, 53-54
    increase in, xvii
    police concerns about, 53-54
    and stalking, 35
    and substance abuse, 60-61. *See also* active attackers
visitor logs, 144, 145
visitor policy, 20, 143-45
voice and vocal tone, 9, 79

warnings, 33, 74
Waterman, Bob, 17
weekly inspection tasks, 140
Welfare and Institutions Codes, 55
What Shamu Taught Me about Life, Love, and Marriage (Sutherland), 67, 68
Whisper, Assertive, 9
White, Condition, 2
Wining, Jim, 79-81
withdrawal, 39
witnesses:
    and citizen's arrests, 83
    colleagues as, 145
    and emergencies, 126
    and harassment, 31
    and reporting abuse, 77
    in Security Incident Reports, 138
women:
    gender differences in perception of safety, 1-2
    gender ratios of staff, 1
    and harassment, xviii, 29-36
    staring at, 71-72
working alone strategies, 86, 88-92

Yellow, Condition, 2
Yes, No, Maybe people, 6-7, 12
"yes, and" *vs.* "yes, but," 10-11

About the Author

Since 2000, **Dr. Steve Albrecht** has made himself well known to library training audiences around the country. He has trained thousands of library employees, live and online, in service, safety, and security. He has worked with city and county libraries, K-12 libraries, college and university libraries, special libraries, and law libraries, in more than thirty states.

Steve holds a doctoral degree in business administration (DBA), an MA in security management, a BA in English, and a BS in psychology. He is board certified in human resources, security management, employee coaching, and threat assessment.

He has written twenty-four other books on business, security, criminal justice, and leadership topics. He lives with five dogs, two cats, and three chickens. (Not all in the same room, of course.)

He can be reached at https://DrSteveAlbrecht.com and AskDrSteve@Library20.com.

www.ingramcontent.com/pod-product-compliance
Lightning Source LLC
Chambersburg PA
CBHW052100300426
44117CB00013B/2219